Life Is a Banquet

www.edwardblom.se/in-english
www.twitter.com/edward_blom
www.youtube.com/edwardblom
www.instagram.com/edward_blom

Photography by Eva Hildén Smith
Graphic design by Wickholm Design Dept.
Other photographs: p. 17 privately owned, p. 61 the Blom family, p. 71 Gunilla Kinn
Blom, p. 82 Björn Markusson, p. 83 Björn Markusson (1), TV3 (2), Ulf Berglund
(3), Elias Österberg (4), Pernilla Thelaus/TV3 (5), p. 184 Gunilla Kinn Blom

Skyhorse Publishing books may be purchased in bulk at special discounts for sales
promotion, corporate gifts, fund-raising, or educational purposes. Special editions can
also be created to specifications. For details, contact the Special Sales Department,
Skyhorse Publishing, 307 West 36th Street, 11th Floor, New York, NY 10018 or
info@skyhorsepublishing.com.

Skyhorse® and Skyhorse Publishing® are registered trademarks of Skyhorse
Publishing, Inc.®, a Delaware corporation.

www.skyhorsepublishing.com

10 9 8 7 6 5 4 3 2 1

Library of Congress Cataloging-in-Publication Data is available on file.

Print ISBN: 978-1-62914-700-0
Ebook ISBN: 978-1-63220-026-6
Cover design by Owen Corrigan
Skyhorse edition edited by Constance Renfrow and Amy Li

Printed in the United States of America

Life Is a Banquet

A Food Lover's Treasury of Recipes, History, Tradition, and Feasts

Edward Blom

With assistance from Gunilla Kinn Blom

Photography by Eva Hildén Smith

Translated by River Khan

Skyhorse Publishing

Contents

Dear Reader,

I am so happy that my first cookbook now exists in English and will therefore be accessible to an international audience!

In Sweden, I am a gastronomist and food historian, well-known from TV and other media platforms. In the English-speaking world, I hope that my recipes and stories will be appreciated in their own right. Some of the dishes I present here are my inventions; others are my interpretations of culinary classics, while some are collected from friends, family and historical cookbooks. The Swedish cuisine dominates, but German, British, American, French, and Asian cooking are also important sources of my inspiration. My wife, Gunilla, and I love to entertain guests. So we are very proud that the Gourmand World Cookbook Awards jury—the "Oscars of food awards"—gave this book a second prize in the Best Entertaining Cookbook–category earlier this year.

Welcome to our culinary universe, and remember: life is indeed a banquet!

Edward Blom
Stockholm, October 2014

Editor's Note:

American unit conversions have been added throughout this book for the ease of the user. Every effort has been made to keep the measurements exact. In some cases, the cook may wish to round off a measurement for convenience. We leave this up to the judgment of the cook. When baking or making sauces it is best to stick to the exact measurements to ensure success, but for most cooking, slight variations in ingredient amounts will still yield delicious results.

My love for food!

For as long as I can remember, I have loved food. When I was three years old, my mother walked in on me heating frozen buns in the oven all by myself with the explanation that: "It's tastier this way" . . . When I was six years old, Grandpa resolutely put a padlock on the pantry, and my favorite game of "Pantry boy" (where, sitting beneath my sister's desk, I filled Dixie cups with different combinations from the pantry and ate one after the other) ended forever.

With seven years to my name, I shocked the school doctor when, during a conversation about my weight, he asked what my favorite dishes were and I recited: "Crab, crayfish, filet mignon, Veal Oscar, plaice, bami goreng, cheese fondue, port wine marinated roast beef—and above all the large cheese buffet at the Hotel Anglais!" The doctor (who thought all children answered that question with what they were used to eating, and not what the greatest food experiences of their lives had been) looked at my father in astonishment and asked: "How are you managing your household finances?"

For just as long as I have been passionate about food, I have been fascinated by how the flavors and consistencies develop in the kitchen. My dad in particular allowed me to take part in the cooking, even when I was a small, messy child. When I reached school age, I learned from Grandma the mysteries behind old-fashioned home cooking. Sometimes even Mom would let me take part, even though she had the responsibility of day-to-day cooking and therefore had less patience.

From around ten years of age I was fascinated by cookbooks, a couple of specimens of Sweden's *Allt om mat (All About Food)* magazine, and the odd cooking show that existed in those days (the best was a black and white rerun where Erik "Bullen" Berglund, a classic Swedish food expert, described how to fry entrecote). I gladly locked myself in the kitchen for hours on Saturday nights, and then the family was invited to a multicourse dinner. For my parents, I would have brought up at least one bottle of "Larsen's express wine" from the cellar and had frothed milk for the cappuccino. And since then, I've kept going. I've cooked food for large parties, made cheese fondue over a fire pit at medieval reenactments, made seven-course feasts in student dorm kitchens, read cookbooks, visited restaurants, copied, tested, and experimented.

After almost ten years as a student in the humanities, I started working at Sweden's Center for Business History in 1997. Since then, the historical aspects of food and drink have come into focus even more. I have researched and written about breweries, dairies, Swedish arrack punsch, the grocery business, city hotels, and much more. The past five or six years I've also made quite a few TV and radio appearances about cooking and food history, but more about that on p. 80. I give lectures and write articles about everything from *smörgåsbord* to pea soup, and I also combine lectures with tastings of arrack punsch, spiced brännvin, or cheese.

I am, however, not a trained chef and have never worked at a restaurant. I can indeed create lovely flavors but I often use the wrong terminology, am unaware of many things professionals view as self-evident, and I always leave the kitchen in chaos when I'm done. But this has its advantages—one of which is that my recipes are created in regular, cramped kitchens with only the basic equipment. So don't blame outside circumstances; with enough dedication, you too can prepare these dishes! My goal is that everyone who uses this book will experience the same joy I do when I am enjoying cooking and eating my favorite dishes.

Edward Blom

Edward Blom
Stockholm, Spring 2013

Directions

A useful piece of advice is to read through the whole recipe before buying the ingredients, and especially before you start making the dish, so you know exactly what you are getting yourself into. At the bottom of each recipe, I will often include suggestions for accompaniments; these are not always included in the list of ingredients and I may not have given the recipes for them. This is because I've made the assumption that you have access to a basic cookbook and/or the Internet. Further, I will not be explaining every step in detail, down to directions for "how to whip cream."

The quality of the raw ingredients varies. Particularly when it comes to seasoning, you shouldn't take the measurements as gospel truth. If you've added a bouillon cube with high salt content, you may need to cut the amount of salt used in half, and if the spice container has been sitting on the shelf for five years, you may need to use more. A large clove of garlic can weigh more than twice that of a small one. This is why you have to trust your taste buds and take the exact measurements with . . . a pinch of salt. At the same time: don't be too self-willed. You can't just omit an ingredient, halve the amount of cream, or skip a step just because you don't understand its role. Even small adjustments can completely change the end result. If you want to try my dishes, you must also follow my recipes. Although, I've almost certainly made mistakes in a few places, so make sure to check www.edwardblom.se/in-english for extra tips and corrections.

The recipes have been made using a convection oven; the temperatures may need to be increased by 20–25°C (35–40°F) for a conventional oven. The portions have been exaggerated, but even so, I presume that you will do as I do and eat a whole menu with appetizer, main course, dessert, and/or cheese. The goal is for you to be well and truly full!

The dishes in my cookbook are not diet food, but I would argue the food is both is healthy and good for you. Like many others, I too strive to maintain control over my weight and health. For the past fifteen years, I've been following the French low-carb diet, the Montignac Method (with exceptions for beer and small doses of arrack punsch). Therefore, all the dessert recipes have been created with sugar substitutes, though I've also included how much sugar that equates to. Many people who have read the manuscript think it's ridiculous to recommend the use of sugar substitutes, but if you follow a low-carb diet or have problems with your sugar intake, then you'll appreciate it.

Many of the recipes call for Swedish ingredients. Some of them might be difficult to purchase in the United States, but substitutes have been listed wherever possible. You can find Swedish food and drink items in web shops and specialty stores—particularly in New York, Chicago, Minneapolis, and other parts of "Swedish America"—but much is also available in Ikea's food stores all over the world.

In particular, there are three special ingredients that I love and use a lot:

• *Ansjovis*—Swedish anchovy fillets, which are not anchovies at all but really fermented, sweetened, and spiced sprats. They constitute a fantastic spice and give any stew or sauce a great umami taste.

When used as fish (see p. 16 and 188) ansjovis can be substituted with pickled herring; when used as a spice, you can substitute with anchovies or Worchestershire sauce. But do try to get hold of a jar or two; you can buy Swedish anchovy fillets in specialty stores, or at Ikea under the name *skarpsill* (Swedish for sprats).

• Lingon or lingonberries (pg. 109)—lovely little tart berries from the deep Scandinavian forests; a staple in the traditional cooking of Northern Europe and excellent as a bitter spice or as a preserve. Mountain cranberries or cowberries are American equivalences; red currants or cranberries are okay as more accessible substitutes.

• Swedish punsch—which has indeed been distributed in the United States for a few years (under the brand names Kronan and Carlshamn). You may also blend it yourself, with sugar, squeezed lemon, and Batavia arrack.

In general, I recommend using the recipe's metric measures for the most exact result. Also, make sure to watch some of the recipes come alive on my YouTube channel: youtube.com/edwardblom—and do follow me on social media (see p. 2).

Most important of all: have fun while cooking!

A traditional Swedish Brännvinsbord

Back in sixteenth-century Sweden, it was common practice to provide guests with a small table of bread, butter, cheese, and beer; these were meant to be eaten before the proper meal commenced. From the 1600s onward, the *brännvin* (brännvin is the Swedish term for spiced vodka, i.e., liquor distilled from potatoes or grain) became such an important part that it actually came to be named the "*brännvinsbord*" or "snaps table." Transportation was arduous and several hours could pass between the arrival of the first and last guest. The brännvinsbord became a pleasant diversion while waiting for others. It was wonderful to take a warming nip of liquor upon coming in from the cold and to take a small morsel to keep up one's blood sugar level before the real dinner began—a little like today's chips and dip and starter drinks.

The food was soon embellished with a few small dishes such as herring salad, fried pork, or some cold meats and, by the start of the 1800s, the brännvinsbord could consist of ten to fifteen dishes. There were at least three varieties of brännvin, often poured into beautiful crystal carafes.

Sadly, the ladies were often excluded. In a few rare places in the country, there were occurrences where the womenfolk were allowed to look on as the men ate. However, by the 1700s, it had become customary for the ladies of the house and the female guests to withdraw to their own private room and drink coffee and liqueur.

People never sat at the brännvinsbord but rather ate standing or sat down on a chair somewhere else in the room. "You weren't supposed to drink more than 'a whole,' 'a half,' and 'a

INGREDIENTS FOR PRODUCING SAUSAGE MAKING

third,'" according to etiquette—there was a whole dinner still to come, after all.

I think the brännvinsbord is too wonderful a custom to let fall into oblivion. When I give lectures, I often arrange for this kind of a table. People love the cold dishes, the foaming beer, and to have a little spiced snaps warm the belly.

Directions

Serve crisp bread, a rustic, soft rye bread (preferably made of sourdough), a really delicious butter (preferably homemade), and a couple of Swedish cheeses at room temperature, like Västerbotten cheese, Prästost cheese, caraway cheese, or other semi-hard cheeses.

Fry pork and serve it cold, possibly seasoned with a little allspice or sage.

Accompany with some kind of herring—herring salad made from salted herring is the classic, but a jar of pickled herring will also do, even if pickled herring appeared only in the late 1800s. Bring out a few varieties of flavorful beer, and at least three varieties of traditionally spiced brännvin—preferably in crystal carafes (or possibly a aquavit container, if you have one). Add your choice of the following accompaniments: old-fashioned smoked salami; smoked or cured salmon or gravlax; a plate with chopped onion, cucumber, and beetroot; a few more varieties of herring and herring salads; anchovies; small sausages (see recipe p. 17); sliced, salted radish; cured lamb leg; cured ham; gentlemen's delight (see recipe p. 16); lobster mayonnaise; cold, sliced ox tongue; smoked goose; cold beef patties with onion and pickled, fried gherkin; eel (preserved, smoked, or in jelly); smoked reindeer or venison with horseradish sauce and pickled herring.

Spiced brännvin snaps

When I was fifteen, my two cousins and I cooked a Russian three-course dinner for our families. In the cookbook we borrowed from the library, there were two recipes for vodka that were quickly flavored overnight with lemon peel and black tea. The lemon peel vodka tasted like Absolut Citron, and this is where my interest in making spiced liquor began. There have been times when I've been so engaged that I even dug up rhubarb roots in friends' gardens, grown my own varieties of wormwood, and searched through shops abroad for exotic spices.

Infusing your own *brännvin* really is not difficult and is a hobby that many more people should discover. The basic principle is that plant pieces are put in a glass jar, and then you pour in regular, unseasoned liquor until the plant pieces are fully covered. Put the lid on. Ideally, it should then be left standing for about a week, but that depends a little on what you have used as flavoring. Any remnants of the plant or flavoring are sifted away and the liquid you have left is what makes up the essence.

With this essence, you can then flavor a good-sized bottle of unflavored liquor a little at a time until enough of the flavor emerges. I think it tastes best if you dilute the liquor down to about 30 percent alcohol beforehand; that way, you can always indulge in an extra glass. Finally the liquor is stored—preferably for five years, but at the least for one month.

Besk

Pick whole wormwood twigs in August when the small yellow flowers are fully developed. If you aren't going to use them immediately, hang them up to dry. Strip off the flowers and the leaves

INGREDIENTS FOR SPICED BRÄNNVIN

(or just the flowers, if you have the patience to be that meticulous) and place them in a jar. Just make sure you don't use the twigs, which create a bad taste. Let stand for a week, covered in liquor, before sifting the plant parts away. Wormwood essence is really strong, so only a small percent (3 percent or so) of the essence will be enough for the liquor.

Hirkum pirkum

St. John's wort is harvested when the buds are about to flower. They don't dry well and should be cut directly into a glass jar with a little liquor. Let stand for three days, sift, and use about 10 percent essence. (St. John's wort is sold in capsule form as a natural antidepressant but has been shown to nullify the effect of many medicines in that form—even contraceptive pills—so be careful with large doses.)

Banquet aquavit

Aquavit is a type of brännvin that, according to European Union regulations, must contain cumin and/or dill seeds and at least 37 volume percentage of alcohol. Other spices that may be used are fennel, coriander, and aniseed.

A spot of sherry, whiskey, or bitter orange peel isn't unusual either.

If you wish to create your own favorite mixture, it's wise to make essences from several different spices and then drop in as much as you want of each variety to be included. You can test it drop by drop in a small glass of liquor. I created the "banquet aquavit" (which I made for the Swedish TV series *Edward Blom's Banquet*) from fresh coriander, fresh fennel crowns, and dried cumin, and I let it stand for a week before sifting. I then used about 5 percent essence.

Also see my wedding snaps on p. 150

Favorite gentleman's delight

There are a lot of variations on this classic Swedish egg and anchovy salad:
Gubbröra or gentleman's delight.
This is my favorite. Potatoes, caviar, and dairy products are—with all due respect—fine, but if you add such things, it stops being a gentleman's delight!

4 APPETIZER PORTIONS

1 regular-sized yellow onion
3 large eggs (or 4 small ones)
butter
1 tin of Swedish anchovy fillets or *"skarpsill"* (4. oz / 125 g) + a little of the liquid
1 egg yolk
approx. 1 tbsp finely chopped dill (frozen is fine)
approx. 1–2 tbsp chives (should be fresh and finely cut)
a dash freshly ground black pepper (optional)
4 slices of dark rye bread or German wholegrain bread

Directions

Chop the onion extremely fine. Hard boil the eggs. Let the eggs cool somewhat in cold water, peel, and chop finely with an egg slicer. Fry about half of the onions in plenty of butter until shiny.

Stir together the eggs, onions, and anchovies cut into pieces.

Add a little of the anchovy liquid and the egg yolk and the dill. Let stand in fridge.

Serving

Serve on buttered rye bread and sprinkle lots of chives (or dill) on top. The gentlemen's delight becomes really gray in color, so the green seasoning is required for cosmetic purposes.

Serve with beer and chilled snaps.

THE DISHES ON THE BRÄNNVINSBORD

1. pickled, fried herring 2. Swedish anchovy fillets 3. anchovies 4. herring salad with cheese 5. pickled herring 6. round smoked eel
7. smoked salmon 8. dried ham 9. dried beef 10. chopped cucumber, onion, and beetroot
11. gentlemen's delight (see recipe above) 12. sliced white radishes 13. smoked sausage 14. banquet sausage (see recipe)
15. cured lamb leg 16. cold, fried pork 17. ground beef patties 18. crisp bread 19. butter 20. sourdough bread
21. cheese 22. porter, pilsner, and ale 23. brännvin with myrtle, St. John's wort, and other spices 24. apples

Traditional banquet sausage

I created this recipe for my TV show, *Edward Blom's Banquet*, from a number of historical recipes. The goal was that it was going to taste like the sausage made in Sweden prior to the mid-1800s. Swedish sausage used to be very strongly spiced, but then (as improvements in preservation led to less rancid meat) became more mild. There are certainly tastier sausages out there, but I think that everyone who likes sausage should try this to get in touch with Sweden's cultural heritage.

The creation itself on TV was a catastrophe: the producers had not arranged for a meat grinder so I had to borrow one from a neighbor of the house we were renting in the village of Gladsax. It had lost its power button, so someone got it started with a pair of pliers—unfortunately, in the wrong direction, so the knives must have been moving backward!

It took me three hours to grind the meat and, by then, there were splashed stinking guts everywhere. After stuffing and simmering the sausages, I was finally supposed to sit down to eat them.

They smelled heavenly. That's when one of the crew discovered that the plastic rod used to push down the meat was only half as large as it had been before. I had managed to grind down more than 3 ounces of plastic into the paste! A whole day's work, and the sausages went straight into the trash.

1.1 lbs (500 g) pork (for example pork loin)
1.1 lbs (500 g) beef (such as chuck)
1–1¾ lb (500–750 g) fat (pure, white fat)
½ lb (250 g) mixed organs (especially kidney and heart, possibly lung, and maybe some liver—but not too much)
1 large red onion
4–5 garlic cloves, crushed
1⅓ tbsp salt (that is 1 tbsp and 1 tsp)
¾ tbsp white pepper
just over ½ tbsp dried, ground ginger
1 heaping tsp lightly crushed mace
1 tbsp marjoram
½ tbsp ground cloves
1–1½ tbsp savory
Just about ½ tbsp allspice
1 beer (should be medium dark and top-fermented, like English ale, but porter will work too)
½–¾ cup (100–200 ml) pig's blood if you prefer a plumper sausage (optional)

Directions

Chop the meat, fat, and organs into pieces, and grind this with red onion and garlic twice in a meat grinder. Add spices, beer, and if you like, pig's blood. When the forcemeat is ready, test-fry a small meatball in a frying pan and taste if it is sufficiently salted and spicy—it should be really spicy. Let the forcemeat rest in the fridge for a couple of hours.

Stuff the sausage loosely into the casing. Bind between each sausage with twine—or tie them, if you can.

Simmer the finished sausages carefully until cooked through (about 20 minutes). They'll benefit from lying in brine first for 24 hours in the fridge or will be even better acidified, smoked, and dried lightly before cooking.

Me with Rasmus Åkerblom at the sausage catastrophe in Gladsax.

Note

If you want to do as they did in the old farming communities of Sweden, you're supposed to shout indecencies and rhymes at the sausages while they're simmering to prevent the skin from bursting, as the ethnologist Jan-Öjvind Swahn told us when we recorded *Edward Blom's Banquet.*

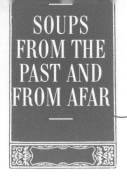
Mexican cheese and chili soup

I was served the model for this soup at a wonderful restaurant in Mexico City in 2003. What got me, apart from the fact that it was really delicious, was the presentation of two completely different soups that complemented each other. You could sip on the chili soup, which was a little too hot, and then quench the fire with the cheese soup. Or start with the cheese soup, which in itself was a little too stodgy, and then freshen your palate with the chili soup. Finally, take a spoon with half of both and just enjoy. . . . After a few attempts at home in Stockholm, I managed to create a recipe that is certainly not identical, but gives a similar result.

--- 6 LARGE APPETIZER PORTIONS ---

The green chili soup

5-25 large green chilies (depending on strength)
2 large, green bell peppers
1 fairly large squash (1 lb / 500 g)
a couple of shallots
1 garlic clove
3⅓ cups (800 ml) mild vegetable stock (broth)
2 slices of white bread, without crusts
approx. ½-1 tsp salt
⅓ cup (75 ml) heavy cream

Directions

Wash the vegetables. Remove the seeds and the pith of 3–5 of the chilies. Coarsely chop them and all the other vegetables. If there's time, fry them quickly in oil to intensify the flavor.

Bring the stock to a boil. Add in the vegetables and cook until they're soft. Add the bread and blend with an immersion blender until smooth.

Blend a couple of raw chilies separately. (If they're extremely mild, keep the seeds and pith for a stronger flavor. Otherwise remove it.)

Add the raw chili one spoonful at a time until the soup is a beautiful shade of green and so strong that it feels slightly too hot to be enjoyably consumed without the accompaniment of the cheese soup. Since there are a lot of varieties of green chili, and they are of completely different strengths, you may need as few as 2 or as many as 25. Add salt to taste.

When the cheese soup is ready, add cream to the chili soup and bring to a boil.

The cheese soup

1¼ cups (300 ml) whole milk
1⅔ cups (400 ml) whipping cream
1 tbsp wheat flour
1½ lbs (700 g) aged cheese, sliced or grated
1 large garlic clove
a little caraway, paprika, and/or nutmeg to taste

Directions

Bring cream and milk to a boil. Thicken the sauce by stirring the flour in a little milk until it becomes a loose paste. Pour this through a fine meshed sieve into the cream mixture while whisking vigorously. Simmer for a moment.

Add the cheese. Whisk as it melts. Do not let it boil!

Add a crushed garlic clove and add spices to taste. (These should not be recognizable in the end result but contribute to the overall flavor.)

The consistency should be medium thick. If it's as thick as fondue, dilute with a little cream and milk; if it's too runny, add a lot more cheese.

Serving

Fill the soup plates just over halfway with the cheese soup and less than halfway with the chili soup.

Note

My youngest niece, Berenike, suggests that you should write the names or initials of your guests with the green soup in the yellow cheese soup and use the plates as place cards.

Cullen Skink

This soup originated among the Scottish fishermen and was made of the day's catch and leftover potatoes. Over time, the recipe has been refined. I personally experienced a delightful variant at a gastropub in Buckinghamshire, England, about seven or eight years ago. Because of that soup, I now bring smoked haddock back on the flight home every time I visit England. Just last year, I was served Cullen Skink as an appetizer at a fabulous wedding reception in Dunblane in the Scottish Highlands.

6 APPETIZER PORTIONS OR 3-4 MAIN COURSE PORTIONS

1 lb (500 g) fillet of smoked haddock
2 yellow onions
6 whole cloves
1 bay leaf
3 whole white peppercorns
2 cups (450 ml) milk
²⁄₃ cup (150 ml) fish stock
3 potatoes
1 small leek
3-4 tbsp butter
1 cup (250 ml) cream
salt, white pepper
some chopped chives or parsley

Directions

Cut one of the onions into wedges and stuff them with the cloves. Add the onion into a pot together with the bay leaf, a little salt, the peppercorns, milk, and the stock. Bring to a boil.

Peel the potatoes, then add them to the soup and boil for 5 minutes. Add the fish and simmer until it is cooked through (about 5 minutes). Remove with a spoon skimmer and set aside to cool.

Continue to simmer the soup until the potatoes are cooked through, then remove them and mash them immediately into mashed potatoes. Set aside.

Strain away the onions and spices from the broth. Chop the other onion and leek finely. Let them sweat in a covered pot with a lot of butter on low heat for at least 10 minutes or until they are soft. (Do not let them brown.)

Pour the broth and cream over the onion and leek.

Add enough of the mashed potatoes so that the soup gets a nice consistency.

Finally, add the fish pieces. Bring to a boil and add salt and ground pepper to taste.

Serving

Serve in soup plates with a few pats of butter and some chives or parsley sprinkled on top

Note

Getting hold of smoked haddock can be difficult unless you smoke it yourself or have a really enthusiastic fish dealer. Other smoked white fish will work as well—except for smoked salmon.

White wine pairs perfectly, but some varieties are incompatible with the smoky flavor. A wheat beer or Scottish ale is a safer bet.

Eel soup according to Hagdahl

I made this soup when we were recording the eel episode of *Edward Blom's Banquet*.
It was the last day to shoot, and Jan-Öjvind Swahn (see p. 83) had unfortunately fallen ill and couldn't participate. So instead, I got to be a part of an ålagille (an eel feast) out on the coast of eastern Skåne, with the colorful eel fisherman and troubadour Hånsa, with staff from local grocery stores and banks who were there for a corporate event. They were happy to try my historical soup, and it was a great feeling to stand and cook the food outdoors Keith Floyd–style.

— 4-6 APPETIZER PORTIONS —

Directions
Skin the eel (or ask the fish dealer to do it since it is quite tricky), possibly fillet it, and then chop it into pieces.

Melt the butter and fry the flour in it. Add the finely chopped onion and garlic.

Pour in the stock. Add all the other ingredients.

Let cook for a few minutes, possibly skim it as well.

Add the eel pieces and simmer briefly until the eel is cooked through.

Taste to see that the eel is done and the soup is strong enough. It should be a little spicy and quite aromatic.

1 small eel (1 lbs / 500 g)
1.4 oz (40 g) butter
1.4 oz (40 g) flour
1 tbsp onion, chopped
¼ garlic clove
4¼ cups (1000 ml) mild beef stock
2 glasses of port wine (3-4 deciliter / 10-13 .oz)
1 tbsp finely chopped parsley
1 tbsp Worcestershire sauce
1 tbsp soy sauce
zest from ¼ lemon
⅛-¼ tsp cayenne pepper
a pinch of ginger
dash of mace
1 tsp crushed (using a pestle and mortar) mustard seeds
3-4 mashed Swedish anchovy fillets (skarpsill)
2-3 tsp anchovy juice
2-3 tsp salt

Charles Emil Hagdahl published *Kokkonsten* (*The Culinary Arts*) in 1879, which, apart from Cajsa Warg's *Hjälpreda,* is the most important cookbook that has been published in Swedish. Hagdahl set out on a quest of collecting an enormous amount of recipes and spent years in the different kitchens of high society, conversing with housewives and kitchen maids. The result wasn't just a collection of three thousand functional and delicious recipes (37 times more than what is in this cookbook!) but a complete documentation of the art of Swedish cuisine.

Little Baden snail cream soup

One of my favorite places on earth is Gasthaus Adler in Baden. I studied in Freiburg when I was young, and my fraternity has kept this tavern as their local haunt. Out among the wine mountains in Glottertal, since the 1800s. You can sit in the garden, enjoy the warmth and the aromas of the blooming flowers, while looking out over the vineyards and cooling yourself with a wonderful Spätburgunder.

The waitresses wear traditional German clothing and the food, while rustic and rural, is prepared with the finest ingredients and methods—even though there have sadly been some attempts to modernize in recent years, such as serving *tapenade* with the bread instead of *Schmalz* (lard)—unless you protest.

A typical dish I've often enjoyed in Gasthaus Adler is this soup made from herbs that grow in the garden, the wine that is grown on the slopes, the snails that have been pulled from the grapevines, and cream from the cows that graze on the rich meadows of the Black Forest: *Badisches Schneckenrahmsüpple.* For people who haven't dared to sink their teeth into a snail, this is a perfect introduction. Baden dishes have always been given the diminutive form, hence "little"—which is comical, since the portions are usually enormous.

¼–½ cup (50–100 ml) shallots, very finely chopped
2 garlic cloves
2–3 tbsp butter
24 snails (wine mountain snails), okay from a can
1 tbsp wheat flour
¾ cup (200 ml) dry, white, German wine
  (preferably Riesling from Baden)
½–⅔ cup (100–150 ml) mild meat stock
  (preferably pork stock, but also works well
  with mild, diluted chicken or veal stock)
approx. ¼ tsp each of thyme, rosemary,
  and sage
½ tsp marjoram (fresh or dried)
½–1 tsp black pepper
salt to taste (depends on how salty the stock is)
2 cups (500 ml) whipping cream, 40%
2 tbsp fresh parsley, 1 tbsp fresh chives, and
  ½ tbsp fresh dill
1 tbsp Weinbrand or cognac
flavoring options: a little grated nutmeg, 1 tsp
  squeezed lemon juice, a little ground cay
  enne pepper

Directions

Chop the onion finely. Fry it in plenty of butter in a pan for at least 10 minutes until soft and transparent—do not allow to brown.

Cut the snails into four pieces each and fry along with the onions for a couple of minutes. Sprinkle some flour on top and stir into the butter.

Pour in the wine, liquid from the can (if you use canned snails), and the stock.

Use a mortar and pestle to grind the dried spices and a little salt and then add it all to the soup.

Add the cream, bring to a boil, and then simmer 20–30 minutes.

Finely chop the fresh herbs and let them simmer for a moment at the end. Add the liquor.

Taste to see if there's more salt needed or possibly any other seasoning.

Note
If you don't have all the herbs at home, it's alright to use fewer varieties; just be sure to keep the same total amount. But the more varieties you use, the richer the flavor.

Added complexity
If you want to avoid the flour, you can use an egg yolk at the end instead—tastier and lower GI, but a little tricky to get right.

Oktoberfest

An ode to beer

I love beer! I love beer with all my heart and every taste bud. For its taste, for its body and fullness, for its tradition and history, for its frothy, soft foam, and for its great variety.

There's beer flowing in my veins as well: my grandmother's grandfather's uncle, Franz Adam Bechmann, came from an old family of German brewers. He came to Stockholm from Bamberg in 1843 and brewed the first bottom-fermented beer in Sweden, upon which he started the entire modernization of Sweden's brewing industry. Apparently even Queen Josephina herself made the switch to his breweries and stopped importing beer from Bavaria, where she grew up. My grandmother's grandfather, Georg Sellman, was taught by Bechmann and another uncle. Later, together with Frans Heiss, he launched pilsner in Sweden.

I was introduced to pilsner as a fifteen-year-old during an Easter I spent with a Catholic youth club in what was then the DDR (East Germany). Before that I had only had cocktails and wine—beer is not for kids. As a sixteen-year-old, I developed a taste for ale and stout after a month in Shropshire. The university year I spent in Germany in 1989–1990 taught me to love Weissbier. Back in Sweden, it became Trappist beer—and porter is, of course, something I already liked as a small kid, when I snuck a taste of it during wort bread baking.

When I was a teenager, the Munich beer gardens and German festivals became dear to me, and not a year has passed by since I became of legal age that I haven't sat in a Biergarten for a day. Oktoberfest beer isn't really sophisticated, but it's perfect for quaffing from a liter tankard while partying. And it's not just the beer I love! I love the traditional Bavarian dirndls and lederhosen, the long tables, Oompah bands, great pork knuckles, cheese stirred with butter, enormous pretzels, rural Catholic piety, gaiety, and *everything* that belongs with Bavaria. In these pages, I'm offering my own little Oktoberfest with four dishes that are fantastic with a big tankard of beer!

Jonas Mann, Gunilla Kinn Blom, Anna Mann, Matts Hildén, and Edward Blom

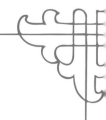

Obazda

Only the Germans could come up with the idea of mixing camembert
with butter to make it even fattier. *Obazda* means "mashed together." The dish was invented
in a biergarten that had a lot of leftover camembert.
Few things taste as good with beer or are as enticing when the infamous drunk munchies set in.

10½ oz (300 g) very mature or even over-mature
    camembert (as fat as possible, at least 45%)
about 5⅓ oz (150 g) butter (if the cheese is
    really strong and over-mature, add some
    more butter)
1–2 tbsp Weissbier
1 tbsp whipping cream, optional
a tad bit of salt (unless the butter and cheese
    are salty enough), optional
¼ tsp white pepper
1 tsp caraway
2 tsp paprika powder
1 small onion

Directions

Mash the camembert (including the rinds) with the
butter.
   Stir with the beer, cream (optional), and the
spices (but save half of the paprika for later) into
an even paste.

Serving

Serve on a platter with the rest of the paprika
sprinkled on top and sliced raw onion.
   Eat with a fork with brezelen (soft pretzel) or
regular pretzel sticks.
   Dip rye biscuits in the obazda, or spread the
obazda in a thick layer on coarse bread.

Note
Soak the sliced onion in cold water for half an hour before using to
get a slightly milder flavor.

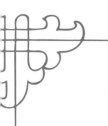
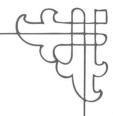

Sliced white radishes

This is one of the most traditional Oktoberfest dishes:
real Bavarians love this hyper-healthy beer accompaniment
at least as much as sausages and pork knuckles.

Directions

Peel a white radish, slice thinly, and serve on a platter. Sprinkle the slices with salt; they should be allowed to "cry" for a moment, after which they are ready to be served.

Alsatian sausage salad (ELSÄSSER WURSTSALAT)

Wurstsalat is the go-to lunch on a hot summer day at a beer fest or in a biergarten.
In Bavaria, however, they serve Nürnberger Wurstsalat, which is made with local sausage.
It becomes Alsatian if you add cheese, and I think that's what you should do.

4 PORTIONS

1²/₃ lbs (750 g) sausage (Berliner sausage, Mortadella, Bologna sausage, or Regensburger wurst)

1 lb (500 g) hard cheese (preferably Emmentaler)

2½–3 yellow onions

²/₃ cup (150 ml) white distilled vinegar (12% is preferred but if you use a vinegar that isn't as strong, simply add more)

about ½ cup (100 ml) neutral flavored oil

¹/₃ cup (75 ml) water

a sprinkling of chives or other green seasoning (mostly for the sake of color)

¼ tsp freshly crushed black pepper

1½–2½ tsp salt

possibly 2–3 finely chopped pickled gherkins (preferably sugar free)

Directions

Cut the onion into very thin slices and put them in a preserving juice made of oil, vinegar, water, spices, and salt and let stand for 5 minutes.

Cut the sausage and cheese into fine strips and stir in. Possibly add pickled gherkins.

Let stand for at least an hour in the fridge. Pour away any excess liquid before serving.

Wurstsalat should have a strong bite of vinegar to it—if it doesn't, add more vinegar.

Serve with coarse peasant bread.

Haxe with sauerkraut stew

When I studied in Freiburg, we would often party for half the night and would eventually get hungry. Fortunately there was Hotel Löwen, open until three in the morning, and Haxe (roasted pork knuckle) was their specialty. Normally pork knuckle is eaten with sauerkraut and dumplings, but Löwen also served an unholy alliance of french fries and béarnaise sauce! We had a deal with a local taxi company that did the ordering and would then arrive at our frat house with a box of Haxe, a cardboard box of fries, and a large bucket of béarnaise for dipping the pork knuckles in.

———————— 4 GIANT PORTIONS ————————

Haxe

4 fresh pork knuckles (not cured,
    at least 2¼ lbs / 1 kg each)
1 beer
water
1 tsp caraway
2 tsp white pepper
2 cloves
5 bay leaves
2 tsp lightly crushed juniper berries
2 large onions, peeled and wedged
1–2 tbsp concentrated beef or vegetable stock
    salt, approx. 1½–2 tsp / quart (4½ cups / liter)
    of water

Directions

Bring the beer and water, mixed with the spices, onion, and stock, to a boil. Add the pork knuckles, pour in enough water to cover, salt, and return to a boil.

    Simmer for 1½ hours.

    Remove the pork knuckles (but save the broth). Roast them on a rack above the roasting pan in the oven on 250–350°F (125–175°C) for another 1–1½ hours. Turn a couple of times and pour a little of the broth on top at regular intervals so the rind gets crispy.

    The Haxe are done when they are a beautiful golden brown and crispy and the meat comes away easily and is not hard to chew. You could also grill them toward the end of their cooking time if they are not crispy enough.

Note

This recipe requires a very large pot, but you can also distribute the pork knuckles among several pots. The broth from the cooked pork knuckles is perfect to use in many other recipes—the sauerkraut on the next page, for instance. Pork bouillon is difficult to come by.

Dumplings (if they're available) should be served with the Haxe and sauerkraut stew. Since the salt doesn't penetrate the entire Haxe, you'll need to add a little salt at the table.

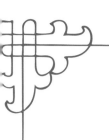

Sauerkraut stew

If you are as fond of sauerkraut as I am, you should double the recipe so there's enough for four.

a large can of sauerkraut
¼–½ cup (50–100 ml) butter
smoked pork (a piece of approx. ½ lb / 250 g)
pork broth
beer, optional
½ tbsp whole caraway seeds
½ tbsp lightly crushed juniper berries
a couple of apple wedges, optional
some sausages, optional
a little bit of lard or grease, optional

Directions

Melt the butter in an iron pot. Chop the smoked pork and fry it up in the butter. (The rind should be cut off but can be allowed to cook alongside as a flavor enhancer.)

Add the sauerkraut and fry it for a moment while stirring—some of it can almost get a little burnt. Pour in a cup or two of liquid, ideally the Haxe broth, and even some beer.

Add caraway, juniper berries, possibly some apple wedges, and a couple of delicious sausages.

Simmer slowly until the water has evaporated and the sauerkraut is soft and nice, which takes 20–40 minutes. If the stew isn't creamy enough, add some lard or grease at the end.

Christmas lasts until Easter

Thus goes an old Swedish Christmas song. Christmas begins on the 24th of December and steams ahead at full force until Twelfth Day, Epiphany Day, fades slowly out to Twentieth day Knut, when Christmas is danced out, but it still isn't completely over until Candlemas. During the days of Christmas you're ONLY allowed to eat Christmas food! Excepting New Year's day and weddings. Some think that this sounds monotonous, but that's because they 1. already started eating Christmas food during advent and 2. don't realize that there's an infinite variety of Christmas food. Here are some of my Christmas favorites.

Allan Hedberg's mumma

Braunschweiger Mumme (or Brunswick Mum) was originally a German beer that was brewed to allow sailors to take beer with them to the tropics without it souring. Therefore, it was "extra everything": extremely malty, dark roasted, sweet, alcohol heavy, and sometimes with added juniper berries and more. Some bottles found their way up to Sweden, and our national bard Carl Michael Bellman even wrote songs about this beverage. Swedes making mumma for Christmas seldom have any clue that what they're really doing is trying to recreate this old, centuries-forgotten German beer. This mumma recipe is the best I've tried. I got my hands on it during my student years; it was given to me by my good friend Joakim, who got it from his grandfather, Allan Hedberg, who played music for films. We improved the recipe by using strong beer instead of regular beer and doubled the amount of Renat brännvin by mistake. (I believe you can increase the Madeira to ²⁄₃ cup / 150 ml). The funny thing is that the result tastes almost like a heavenly *Julmust*—a Swedish Christmas soft drink—but is as strong as wine.

½ cup (100 ml) Renat brännvin vodka
½–²⁄₃ cup (100–150 ml) sweet Madeira
1¹⁄₃ cup (330 ml) Carnegie porter
1¹⁄₃ cup–2 cups (330–500 ml) pilsner
(Staropramen, Jever, or similar)

Directions

Pour the Renat and the Madeira in a pitcher or jug.

Carefully add the porter and then the pilsner.

Note

This mumma is a perfect drink to kick-start a riproaring Christmas party. Flavor-wise it also goes incredibly well with Christmas food and is therefore superb for a Christmas lunch with friends.

In my family, we usually keep the amount of alcohol down during Christmas Eve to give priority to the kids—and to be in a better condition for the midnight mass. So I tend to mix a version based on regular strength porter, regular strength pilsner, and a little splash of Madeira instead.

Feuerzangbowle

Feuerzangbowle is the mild gluhwein's naughty cousin, with stronger spices and definitely a higher alcohol content—and it burns. This punch likely has its roots in the 1700s and would probably, like similar drinks, have been more or less forgotten if it hadn't been for a book and then movie named after the punch. It has attained cult status among German youths who, despite the difficult method of preparation, continue to craft Feuerzangbowle for advent, Christmas, and New Year's celebrations.

2 bottles of unoaked red wine

1 cinnamon stick

at least 1¾ cup (400 ml) dark rum with at least 60% alcohol

5-6 cloves

2 star anise (some people also add other spices, usually nutmeg or ginger, but also bay leaves, juniper berries, black tea, real vanilla, and cardamom)

1 organic orange, cut into thin slices

1 organic lemon, cut into thin slices

1 sugarloaf of about 1 lb (500 g)

Directions

Combine the wine and the spices as well as the sliced citrus fruits. Heat the liquid to just below the point of simmering. Pour the punch into a traditional German punch bowl with tea lights or a burner underneath.

Place a small wire rack over the pot and set the sugar loaf on top.

Heat the rum slightly. Soak the sugarloaf in rum and set it alight. The sugar should burn with a large, blue flame until it has melted completely into the punch.

Continue to pour new rum over the sugarloaf with a metal punch ladle so it continues to burn—but don't pour directly from the bottle, or else it might catch fire! When the sugar has melted, extinguish any remaining fire in the punch.

Note

Feuerzangbowle means Fire Tong Punch and, if you want to be really traditional, you should hold the sugarloaf with fire tongs while it burns instead of placing it on a grate. This does, however, require a very hard sugarloaf.

Sugarloaves are available to purchase in grocery stores in Germany and may be available in German specialty food stores around Christmastime.

If you can't get a hold of rum with 60% alcohol content, then pour ¾ cup (200 ml) of dark rum with 40% alcohol by volume into the punch for flavor. Then pour a different sort of liquor with the right alcohol content over the sugarloaf, such as absinthe or green chartreuse.

Danish leverpostej

I've stolen this recipe from an old Danish cookbook I found in an antiquarian book shop.
The book is simply called *Mad* (Food). I make this paté every Christmas and I never
cease to be amazed at how liver and hard fat can be transformed into something so heavenly.
Danish cuisine is excellent and should get more attention in Sweden and the United States.

2¼ lbs (1 kg) liver
2¼ lbs (1 kg) fatback (can usually be found at butcher's shops or farmers' markets)
a dozen Swedish anchovy fillets (sprats, skarpsill) with some of its juice
2 small, yellow onions
1 tsp black pepper
1 tbsp salt
2 eggs
1 cup (250 ml) whipping cream
slices of fatback or bacon to dress the pan

Directions from *Mad*

The liver should be rinsed and scrubbed, then cut into smaller pieces and so should the fatback. The
fatback should then be run through a meat grinder and mixed with the sliced liver, fish, and onions.
All of this should then be run through the meat grinder eight times more. Stir the spices, eggs,
and cream into the mixture.
The liver paste can be cooked either in small glasses or baked in a large mold for 1½ hours. If desired,
the mold can first be dressed with ⅔ lb (300 g) of fatback that has been cut into thin slices.

Note

It's best to let the pan stand in a water bath (a long pan with a little water) while cooking in the oven on quite
low heat. Some slightly coarser Danish patés are incredible when warm from the meat shop's oven, but this version tastes
best when it's been allowed to cool. The recipe is quite generous, so if you don't want to have a gigantic paté, you can
instead use four or five aluminum pans and give small patés as Christmas gifts.

Edward's Yule ribs

Most of today's Swedish Christmas dishes are fairly modern creations that have come
in the last 150 years, such as ham, meatballs, and pickled herring.
But hearty meat dishes, such as ribs, are as old as time
—but only a prince could have afforded all these spices back then.

4 PORTIONS

approx. 2¼ lbs (1 kg) short ribs

1 onion

1 garlic clove

2–3 tsp salt (depending on the amount of
   liquid)

1 apple

8 prunes

5 cloves

10 allspice berries

a couple of black and white peppercorns

a pinch of mace (or a little grated nutmeg)

a piece of fresh ginger (the size of a thumbnail)

1 tsp Worcestershire sauce

approx. 1 tbsp malt vinegar (can be substituted
   with 1 tsp plain vinegar and 2 tbsp of beer)

1 tbsp soy sauce, Kikkoman, for example

1 tbsp concentrated beef stock

a couple Swedish anchovy fillets (sprats, skarpsill)
   and its juice

approx. 2 cups (500 ml) julmust (Swedish
   Christmas soft drink, available at specialty stores,
   can also be substituted with 0.25l coca-cola and
   0.25l stout) and the same amount of water
   (the amount depends on the size of the
   pot)

Directions

Cut the ribs roughly and vigorously brown them
in a pot with cleaved onion and roughly chopped
garlic. Salt both sides. Throw in the wedged apple,
prunes, spices, and sauces as well as Swedish
anchovies.

Pour in enough julmust and water to cover the
ribs about ⅔ of the way. Simmer over low heat
until the ribs are completely tender, which takes
2–3 hours.

The ribs only gain from being left in their juices
for a day, when they can be warmed and eaten.

Delicious with apple sauce and red cabbage.

Note

The juice produced is delicious as-is (possibly with some corn starch
stirred in to thicken) or as a basis for a sauce.

Creamy fjällfil with ginger snaps

A very Swedish dish made with *fjällfil*—a type of *filmjölk* (or soured milk) beloved in the Nordic countries.
When I was a kid, I used to eat this for lunch during Christmastime.
Here, though, I've changed it into a dessert. This is my favorite dish to serve foreign friends at Christmas.

— 4 PORTIONS —

1 liter *fjällfil*
½–¾ cups (100-200 ml) whipping cream
plenty of homemade pepparkakor
    (or ginger snaps)

Directions
Stir the cream into the *fjällfil*. If it isn't completely smooth, then whisk a couple times.

Pour into dessert bowls and crumble plenty of gingerbread on top.

Note
Fjällfil is a Swedish brand of old-fashioned, thick, viscous fermented milk; more sour than regular Swedish *filmjölk*. Outside of Sweden, you can find *filmjölk* in Whole Foods or specialty stores. Homemade ginger snaps taste much better than the ones available in stores.

Restaurant Provisions Shop, Stockholm

Edward's culinary commandments

1. Taste and don't give up!

No recipe is enough: the difference between decent and delectable is always decided toward the end, when you have to think of what could be missing. A little more strength, fruitiness, sweetness, acidity, fat, or spices? Practice, practice, practice! Let the spoon fly between pot and mouth! Your tongue and nose are your tools—a million times more valuable than any super knife, electric kitchen gadgets, and those gizmos people brag about. Cooking up a recipe and then serving it to your guests without first tasting it is as absurd as a violin maker crafting a violin without ever playing it.

Don't give up: never place an uninspired dish on the table. Try to salvage it. First with fat: butter, duck fat, lard, cream, marrow, and oil. And then, if needed: bacon, wine, garlic, brandy, currant juice, Worcestershire sauce, vinegar, Kikkoman soy sauce, fish sauce, aged cheese, and Tabasco—but probably not all at once.

2. Never throw away food!

Even a tablespoon of peas, half a potato, or the dregs of a meat stew can benefit a breakfast sandwich, an omelet, or a hash.

Save meat and vegetable broth and freeze to use as a base for sauces, soups, and stews. Even the bones, vegetables, and lobster shells, etc. can be frozen to make stock from later. Pour off the bacon fat and use it for frying. And never throw away the juice from Swedish anchovy fillets—it's an amazing flavoring for everything.

3. Don't forget the sauce!

A dish without sauce is like a human being without a soul. Everything benefits from sauce, and the person who attains perfection in sauce making will always have happy guests. This holds true even if you have an Italian cookbook that says you should serve veal without any liquid accompaniment! The rule of sauce is fundamental and goes before any and all national ideas.

4. Browning!

Almost everything becomes tastier when it is browned first. I let almost everything get a good brown surface before it ends up in stews, soups, or gratins.

But for everything you hold dear, use an iron pan: cast iron gives an amazing flavor! Teflon is a neurotoxin.

5. Don't forget the cheese!

A proper meal doesn't just consist of appetizer, main course, and dessert—but also cheese.

6. Close your eyes!

Anyone who has ever said "you eat with your eyes first" was lying; you don't eat with them any more than you eat with your earlobes. Almost all food tastes better the uglier it looks. Take ratatouille, for example. If you pull it off the cooker while it still consists of recognizable, beautiful ingredients, it doesn't taste half as good as when it's become a brown mush.

Focusing on appearance has ruined so many taste experiences. Instead, learn to make real stews, where many ingredients sacrifice themselves for the greater whole over the course of hours of simmering. Yes, it becomes brown, or gruel gray, but it doesn't matter. If worse comes to worst, you eat with a blindfold.

7. Don't cheat!

You can never make good dishes from bad ingredients. You absolutely cannot replace butter with margarine. And use organic butter, as regular butter is no longer high enough quality these days. Cream should be 40 percent; that 36 percent option with additives is vile. Vegetables and fruit taste better when they're organic. Soy sauce should be an authentic brewed soy, which really adds flavor and fullness; to make it less salty, I prefer to use Japanese soy sauce, but the Chinese make some nice varieties, too.

If you can't afford the best of everything, then choose to get really good quality of the things that are already inexpensive to begin with, such as onions and vegetables, or things you only use very little of, such as mustard, spices, etc. Don't cheat with the effort either—cooking is a serious business.

8. Don't be a wimp!

If gelatin, fat, veal heart, sheep eyes, fish that are "looking at you" from the plate, fried pets, etc. gross you out or if you have any other mental block that is stopping you from being able to enjoy a good meal, invest in a couple of therapy sessions and work it all away. Or just bite the bullet, and bite into that sheep's eyeball. It's only you who loses out by being squeamish about something delicious. (I am, of course, not referring to severe eating disorders, which are terrible diseases, but just plain old wimpiness.)

9. Don't be lazy!

If your guests have legitimate reason to pass on certain dishes (such as allergies, sobriety, serious health issues, or religious rules) don't let it hamper you. Limitations inspire creativity. I'll never forget when as a student I was going to cook a three-course meal in my little kitchenette that had just two burners, and one of my guests turned out to be a vegetarian and two were strictly kosher, while I myself was longing for meat and had just started following the Montignac Method. But in the end, everyone was satisfied. It's not all that difficult and, as a host, you have to be willing to sacrifice a little.

But if one of the guests just doesn't care for a certain flavor, then you're welcome to ignore that. Sometimes it actually helps stimulate one's culinary mind to eat something you don't like.

10. Never forget that "much is more"!

Restraint is as terrible in the art of cooking as it is in interior decorating. A fat-free dish is as tedious as a white wall. Think baroque and follow my motto: "It's all delicious and just too much." You'll be a happier person.

Happy Easter

Fasting ends with Easter, when I as a Catholic try to limit
the alcohol, partying, and gluttony. I traditionally celebrate Easter
Eve—the most important day during the Swedish Easter—with relatives,
but on Easter day, it's time for a spring celebration! Which means Easter lunch
at home with a couple of friends, plenty of chilled bottles of German Riesling, lots of food
—and homemade egg liqueur! Here are my absolute best recipes for festive Easter meals.

Tord's egg and herring salad

We celebrate many holidays with my aunt,
both of my cousins, and their families. I got this recipe from Tord,
my cousin Helena's beloved. Quick to make and modern,
but delicious nevertheless.

---

1 small jar of mustard herring (about 1 cup (240 g), chopped
a little bit of mustard herring sauce
2-3 hardboiled eggs, chopped (in an egg slicer)
1 small red onion, finely chopped
¾-1 cup (200-250 ml) crème fraiche

Directions

Stir together all the ingredients in a
jar and add mustard sauce to taste.
Ideally, let it set in the fridge for a day.

Biblical lamb stew with figs and wine

This stew was the last dish we made when Ellen Wästfelt
and I were hosts for one summer of Swedish Radio's cooking show, *Menu*.
The theme was The Last Supper and was about, among other things,
Biblical food as well as the last meal of prisoners. The former is a subject I also give lectures on.
The recipe is originally from a book on this theme, but has been adjusted.

7-8 PORTIONS

3⅓ lbs (1½ kg) lamb meat (weigh the meat with
   any bones removed, but let them boil with
   the meat to provide extra richness and flavor)
3 tbsp olive oil for frying
3-4 garlic cloves
2 cups (500 ml) red wine
1¼ cups (300 ml) water
1 tbsp lightly crushed mustard seeds
1 tbsp lightly crushed coriander seeds
1 tbsp whole caraway
approx. 1-2 tsp salt
1¼ cups (300 ml) dried, roughly chopped figs

Directions

Cut the meat into large pieces and brown them
in olive oil. Crush the garlic and add it to the pan
toward the end of the browning. Add wine, water,
spices, salt, and figs.

Bring to a boil, cover with a lid, and let simmer until the meat is soft and the consistency a bit
syrupy (about 2 hours).

If there's still too much liquid when the meat
is cooked, pour it into a separate pot and reduce
before returning to the original pot.

Sample and add more salt and spices if required.

Serving

Serve with bread and red wine and ideally with
some legumes, hummus, pomegranates, and other
tasty odds and ends. Also delicious with oriental
yogurt, but then it's no longer biblical.

Edward's Easter egg liqueur

Every Easter, I make my own egg liqueur. I don't just serve it with the coffee, but I top the dessert with halved Kinder Surprise eggs filled with the liqueur. The small yellow containers that hold the toys are given to each couple at the table to share and put together.

12-14 egg yolks (depending on size)
6 oz (175 g) sugar or sugar substitute, until just sweet enough
—even with the use of sugar substitute you'll still need 2-3 tbsp of real sugar
$^2/_3$ cup (150 ml) rum or cognac
½ cup (100 ml) unflavored vodka
a splash of Swedish arrack punsch, optional
¼ cup (50 ml) whipping cream
real vanilla extract

Directions
Pour the egg yolks and sweeteners into a food processor and turn on the beater.
Pour in the liquor (while beating) and then pour in the cream.
Add vanilla extract to taste and sample to see if the sweetness and richness are to your liking.
For best results: heat the liqueur in a water bath until it thickens a little (it doesn't need to get too hot).
This will bring out the egg flavor, among others.
The bottled egg liqueur will keep for at least a couple weeks in the fridge.

Tip
When our friends Fredrik and Per made this liqueur, they made a
large batch and found that you can also pour 2 parts boiling water into a cup with
1 part egg liqueur, and presto! You have an egg toddy.

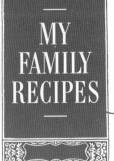
Grandma Karin's golden fried kroppkakor

This was my maternal grandmother's signature dish. During one lifetime, she had managed to perfect the art of making kroppkakor, literally "body cakes"—Swedish dumplings, filled with onions and pork. Often, our entire family gathered in her home in Stockholm and ate and ate while a constant stream of freshly fried kroppkakor were passed from the oven to the dining room. These were drowned in butter and covered with lingonberry jam and the leftover filling, which Grandmother always made a double batch of. Afterward, everyone was knocked out and every couch and guest bed was used for a collective nap—until Grandmother woke us all with coffee and pastries from the Norra Strand Bakery, housed in the same building.

——— 18 KROPPKAKOR (4 LARGE PORTIONS) ———

Kroppkaka dough
3⅓ lbs (1½ kg) potatoes of a mealy variety
   (preferably King Edward, of course)
salt
2 large or 3 small eggs
1¼–2 cups (300–450 ml) wheat flour
a little white pepper

Filling
(DOUBLE THE RECIPE IF YOU ALSO WANT THE FILLING AS ACCOMPANIMENT)
⅓ lb (150 g) cured pork
⅓ lb (150 g) smoked ham
6 tbsp chopped yellow onion
1½–2 tsp allspice

butter for frying and melting
lingonberries, fresh or preserves

Directions
Boil the potatoes in 2 tsp salt per quart of water until almost done.

Drain them immediately and mash them while still warm.

Mix in eggs, flour, white pepper, and about 1–1½ tsp salt. There should be enough flour to make it possible to form buns.

Cut the pork, ham, and onions into tiny pieces. Fry the pork and the onions in a frying pan with plenty of butter; add the ham near the end. Season with allspice.

Form 18 buns from the dough. Create a hollow in each and distribute the filling across each— pinch the sides of the bun together over the filling. Flatten the buns.

Boil a couple at a time, uncovered, in lightly salted water until they float to the top. Then simmer for another 5 minutes. Remove them with a skimmer spoon and let cool.

Fry in butter until they're warm and golden brown.

Serving
Serve with melted butter, lingonberry preserves or fresh lingonberries (may be substituted with red currants or cranberry preserves), and the extra filling.

Note
The kroppkakor are even better if they're boiled the day before, left to rest in the fridge, and fried right before its time to eat them. This also gives you more time to spend with your guests.

Papa James' beef patties

My dad's beef patties are something I strongly associate with my childhood. I remember how I was allowed to take part in making them in the small kitchen of our row house, which we moved away from when I was five. The thing that gives the patties their special character is the large amount of finely chopped onions you stir into the batter. The onion becomes almost blackened on the surface, but inside they're well cooked.

When I was young, dad also poured in bone meal, which was considered healthy for children at the time, but hardly has any culinary benefits. I remember the big cardboard jar decorated with a happy child with shining white teeth. Where dad bought it, I have no idea.

I've never met anyone else who had to eat bone meal as a child—but even today, it's given to dogs and cats, so it's probably healthy.

--- 4 STINGY PORTIONS ---

1¼ lb (600 g) ground beef (at least 15% fat)
1 large onion, finely chopped
2 eggs
1 bunch of parsley, finely chopped, optional
½–1 tsp salt
black pepper, roughly grated or crushed in a mortar
½ cup (100 ml) whole milk or sparkling mineral water
(for health purposes, you're welcome to add 1 tbsp good quality bone meal)
butter for frying

Directions

Put the ground meat in a bowl and mix in all the ingredients, except for the liquid, which is stirred in last. Stir until the paste gets a consistency suitable for shaping patties. (Since the paste contains a lot of onion, it's good to stir it for a long time so the patties stick together better.)

Fry in butter and serve with lingonberries, boiled potatoes, and gravy (see p. 123).

Grandma Astrid's fish soufflé

This was a real festival food at our home.
This was originally my beloved paternal grandmother's recipe, but she never cooked food
during my lifetime, as she lived in a retirement home for the last seventeen years
of her life. Instead, I associate it with my mother.

— 4–6 APPETIZER PORTIONS —

2 cup (400 g) cleaned cod
  (it's okay to use frozen cod, but let it thaw
  and drain first before you weigh it)
2 tbsp butter
4 tbsp flour
½–¾ cup (100–200 ml) milk
1¼–1 ⅔ cup (300–400 ml) juices from the
cooked fish stock
salt
white pepper
3 eggs
breadcrumbs

2–2½ sticks (150 g) butter to melt

Note
When it comes to soufflé, you must ensure it's not waiting on
the guests; rather, the guests must wait for the soufflé, as it will
deflate immediately after it's removed from the oven. Ideally it
should puff up, but that doesn't happen often, and it tastes just
superb anyway.

Directions
Boil the fish and save the juices.

Make a sauce by melting 2 tbsp of butter and stir
in the flour; when it has dissolved, whisk in boiling
milk, then add enough fish juice to make the consistency sauce-like. Add salt and pepper to taste.

Remove the pot from the heat, let cool a bit,
and then whisk in the egg yolks.

Mash the fish with a fork into an even paste
(there should now be 1¼ cups / 300 ml) and stir it
into the sauce.

Let the batter cool.

Whisk the egg whites into a stiff foam and carefully fold them into the paste.

Pour the mix into a buttered, bread crumb
filled soufflé pan. The pan should be tall and
straight, as the soufflé will rise during the baking.

Bake at the bottom of the oven at 350°F
(175°C) 45–55 minutes. Don't open the oven
while baking—it will cause the soufflé to deflate.

Serve the soufflé immediately with lots of
melted butter and cooked green peas.

James and Sylvia "Ninnie" Blom

Aunt Frida's pink potato salad

Frida Sundström was a party cook—not a full-time employed cook in a person's home, but someone who was hired for parties and important dinners. She sometimes showed up at my father's childhood home and took over the kitchen—and out would come the most delicious dishes. More often, he would meet her in his maternal aunt, Irma's, home, where elegant white-tie dinners would often be arranged. During my paternal grandfather's final year (when he was seriously ill with MS), Aunt Frida, would often come and help out, even with regular day-to-day cooking. Dad, his sister, and eventually my mother became very attached to this warm and wonderful woman, whom they continued to visit after she had stopped working—and because of that, Dad was gifted some of her fantastic recipes. This is one of them, and it's actually the most delicious potato salad in the world. And because it's pink, it makes a festive element on the buffet table.

4-6 PORTIONS

approx. 2 lbs (1 kg) potatoes (of the hard variety)
2–3 preserved beetroots (1/3 lb / 150 g)
2 tbsp finely chopped yellow onion
a bunch of parsley
1/4–1/2 pinches of salt
2 tbsp capers
3/4 cup (200 ml) mayonnaise
just about 1/2 cup (100 ml) whipping cream, non whipped

Directions

Boil the potatoes (but don't overcook), and then chill in the refrigerator. Peel and dice the potatoes.

Chop the beetroots into small pieces (1/2 cm at most) and fine chop the onion and parsley.

Combine the potatoes, beetroots, onions, parsley, and capers in a bowl (but save some of the parsley for decoration).

Stir together the mayonnaise, cream, salt, and a spoonful of beetroot juice and then carefully mix all the ingredients together. Let stand a couple of hours.

Pour into a pretty bowl and garnish with chopped parsley.

Aunt Frida in my grandmother's kitchen, after she was widowed and moved to a small apartment in Stora Essingen at the beginning of the 1960s.

Mama Ninnie's avocado mixes

Many of you have probably eaten the avocado appetizer and thought it felt very '80s, but so what? I think it's one of the simplest ways to get a really good starter.
Mom used to make the avocado dessert in the '70s and I thought that one was a little more unusual, until—damn!—something similar suddenly showed up in *The History Eaters* (Swedish version of BBC's *The Supersizers*)! These two dishes probably shouldn't be served during the same dinner—unless you're crazy about avocado.

──────── 4 SMALL APPETIZER PORTIONS ────────

Avocado appetizer

2 ripe avocadoes
¼ lemon, juice
1 yellow onion, finely chopped
2¾–3½ oz (80–100 g) red lump fish roe
¾ cup (200 ml) crème fraiche (or sour cream)
¼ tsp salt
¼ tsp black pepper
8 shrimp

Directions

Run the avocado flesh and the lemon juice through a mixer (or use an immersion blender) into a smooth, even cream.

Stir in the onion, the roe, and the crème fraiche. Add salt and crushed black pepper to taste.

Serve in the avocado shells and garnish with shrimp.

Note
I like to sprinkle in a bit of cayenne pepper in, as well.

Avocado dessert (3-4 PORTIONS)

3 ripe avocadoes (keep four halves of the shell)
1 lemon, juice
1½–3 tbsp sugar
strong citrus liqueur, such as Cointreau

Directions

Run avocado flesh, lemon juice, and sugar through a mixer (or use an immersion blender) into a smooth, even cream. Serve in the avocado shells with a little citrus liqueur on top.

When Edward wanted to serve dog food stew

Edward and I *always* talk about food—always, always, always.
Our friend Cecilia gets so mad at us. I usually love everything Edward cooks,
from Indian curry to pink fig ice cream. But once he promised
me a "delicate" stew, which would have "amazing flavors and ingredients."
I had been looking forward to it all day, but when I entered Edward's kitchen, I was
greeted by a slightly nauseating smell that nevertheless reminded me of something from my childhood.
When I lifted the lid on the pot, it turned out to be lung, liver, heart, kidneys, and marrow.
That's what Mom used to make dog food from when she'd been out hunting!
Anything gross you could think of.
Dog food stew. I refused to eat it.
But Edward was so proud and claimed that he'd taken the recipe from Torgny Lindgren's novel, *Pölsan (Hash)*.
Instead we guests were served a backward dinner. It started with coffee and chocolate,
and then strawberries with whipped cream. Then we had cheese, then dove
—and last of all came herring and snaps. It's wasn't easy to get the herring down
when we were already stuffed to bursting. Even Edward thought so.

Anna von Krusenstierna, friend of Edward's

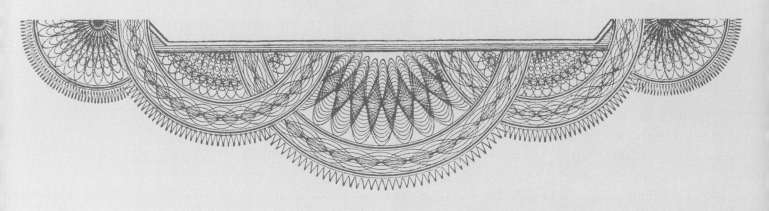

Edward Blom's chicken liver Laphroaig

This dish was born when I wanted to make a chicken liver paté.
The liver was supposed to be fried first, and I wanted to get the paté a little fattier, so I added a lot of butter.
Then, the recipe called for brandy to be added to the paté batter, but I only had whiskey at home
and I distractedly poured it on the liver in the frying pan instead of into the paté batter.
The result was so delicious that I ate almost the entire liver all at once, and the paté had to make do without.

4–6 APPETIZER OR LIGHT SUPPER PORTIONS

¾–1 lb (400–500 g) chicken liver (preferably fresh)
3½ tbsp (50 g) butter
approx. ¾ tsp salt
approx. 1 tsp black pepper, roughly crushed with
    mortar and pestle
at least ⅔ cup (150 ml) very smoky malt whiskey,
    preferably Laphroaig
½–¾ cup (100–200 ml) whipping cream, optional
a slice of bread, optional
duck fat, optional

Directions

Cut the liver into large pieces and fry them in lots of butter until they're almost cooked through.
    Add plenty of salt and pepper.
    Pour in the whiskey and let it cook a bit.
    If you want a more stew-like consistency, you can also pour in a little whipping cream.

Serving

Serve in a small dish like tapas or an appetizer, or even on a piece of toast fried in duck fat. Don't forget to pour on top all the whiskey butter from the frying pan!

Note

If you want to impress your guests, you can do what's shown in the photograph and light the whiskey just after it's been poured over the paté. As Keith Floyd said: not that flambeing affects the flavor much, but it is a lot of fun!

Edwards Köttf...

806 g nötfärs
567 g ananas i spad
ca 2 vitlöksklyftor
Felix och Heinz ketch...
Kines soja
portvin
peppar
oregano
salt

Skala och fi...

Spaghetti sauce from teenage years

I created this spaghetti sauce when I was in high school and prepared it for the entire
St. Erik's catholic youth club at a spring ball. Most liked it, except for an Italian guy
who said that his mother would have thrown it out the window.
It's included here as an example of all the dishes I've made from whatever happened to be in the fridge,
since the age of ten up until today. All the other recipes from this time have been forgotten
—but my sister, Anna Dunér, an author of children's books, received this dish from me on a note
and had written it down in her little recipe notebook as
"Edward's ground beef stew." It's reproduced here in its original form (see picture).

———— 4 PORTIONS (SERVED WITH SPAGHETTI, IT CAN BE ENOUGH FOR MORE) ————

1¾ lbs (806 g) ground beef
20 oz (567 g) canned pineapple
approx. 2 garlic cloves
Felix and Heinz ketchup
Chinese soy sauce
port wine
pepper
oregano
salt

Directions

How the stew was to be arranged was never written down. But the ground beef, as I recall, was fried into crumbs and then I probably added the other ingredients all at once. Then it was most likely allowed to simmer for a little while.

This was served with spaghetti.

The gastronome's pork loin
pork loin in a pleasantly unusual coffee-pepper-wine-sauce

Sometimes coincidence leads to new discoveries.
A few drops of sweet Israeli red left by the sink in
my Stockholm flat wasn't enough when the meat started to stick to the
bottom of the pan, so the cup of cold coffee had to follow.

———— 4–5 PORTIONS ————

6 large slices of pork loin (approx. 2 lbs / 900 g)
5 oz (140 g) bacon, chopped
approx. 1 tsp salt
1½ tsp roughly crushed black pepper
1¼ cup (300 ml) red wine
1¼ cup (300 ml) strong brewed coffee
1¼ cup (300 ml) whipping cream
just over 2–3 tbsp sweet port wine
just over 2 tsp honey
sliced white cabbage, optional
ghee (see p. 113) or butter and olive oil for
   frying

Directions

Fry the pork loin slices and the bacon. Season
with salt and black pepper. Let it get quite hot, so
that the pepper is seared sharply. When the meat
is fully cooked, remove it from the pan.

Pour the wine, coffee, and whipping cream over
the bacon in the frying pan. Season with honey
and salt. Let it cook together into a syrupy sauce
(15–20 minutes). If you like, add some thinly sliced
white cabbage to simmer for the last 5 minutes.

Place the meat (and it's juices) back in the pan.
Let it heat up in the sauce.

Note
You can also try the same sauce with steak, for example a thick skirt
(hanger) steak or flank steak.

Glögg mussels from Harlem

My wife, Gunilla, lived in Harlem, New York, for eleven years.
The first year of our relationship, before she moved back to Sweden,
I stayed with her for long periods of time. We had a great fishmonger around the corner and one day
we bought mussels and a really ugly catfish. This was in December, and I had made different varieties
of mulled wine (or glögg, as it's known in Swedish) for a Christmas party the weekend before.
We had leftovers of the unsweetened version. The result was so good that I wrote it down on
my blog and thus, it survived.

―――――――― 2 PORTIONS, APPETIZER AND MAIN COURSE ――――――――

1 bag of fresh mussels (approx. 2¼ lbs / 1 kg)
½ yellow onion
ghee (see p. 113) or grease and olive oil
2 garlic cloves
5 dried tomato halves
8 slices of bacon
2 tbsp wheat flour
¾ cup (200 ml) glögg (Swedish mulled wine)
   see note
2 fish fillets, preferably catfish, but lumpfish
   can also work
a few splashes of West Indian rum
salt

Me buying catfish at Sea & Sea in Harlem

Directions

Chop the onion finely and fry in plenty of
ghee (or butter) and a splash of olive oil
for about 5 minutes—it should not brown.
Chop the garlic, dried tomatoes, and bacon
and fry for another 5 minutes. Add the bag
of cleaned mussels.

When the mussels gradually begin to open
up, pour in the wine. Let it simmer for a
couple minutes.

Meanwhile, fry the fish fillets in lots of ghee.

Remove the fillets and whisk a couple of
tablespoons of wheat flour into the butter
that the fish has been fried in.

Dilute with the liquid from the mussels,
which should now be removed from the heat.

Bring the sauce to boil, add salt and a little rum
to taste, pour it over the mussels, and stir. Place
the fish fillets on top.

Swedish glögg essence
To make a glögg essence, put these spices in a jar:
1 tablespoon of cardamom kernels, 1 tablespoon of cloves,
1 cinnamon stick, 1 quarter-size piece of dried ginger, maybe a little
lemon zest. Cover with vodka or brandy. Leave the infusion for a week.
Drain. Then add a little of the essence to ¾ cup of red wine, so it gets
spicy and aromatic. (You may want to sweeten it carefully with a pinch
of sugar or substitute.) Infuse more wine to drink some glögg as well—
but heat it first!

When the little ones come to visit

We think it's really nice to occasionally invite our
nieces over for a weekend luncheon without their parents. I have three nieces,
but this time it was only the youngest Berenike (12), who came to visit.
Gunilla's family was represented by her nieces Clara (10) and Astrid (8).
We followed the principle that each child would get what they found scrumptious,
but of a far higher quality than what can be found at the fast food joints.

Pompompom

The luncheon starts with entrance drinks by the piano, of course
—though non-alcoholic. This time we served
Pommac, a Swedish soft drink, with pressed lime, a hearty splash of grenadine,
and frozen raspberries and blackberries.

Purple pommes frites

These pommes frites are made of real potatoes and are fried in duck fat
for a richer flavor. By using Blue Congo potatoes, the pommes frites become purple,
which is popular with our nieces.

Blue Congo potatoes, approx. 1¾ oz (50 g)/child
and ¼ lb (100 g)/adult
enough duck fat to fill a frying pot
salt

Pompompom by the piano. Berenike Dunér, Clara, and
Astrid Kinn visiting Uncle Edward and Aunt Gunilla.

Directions

Peel and cut the potatoes in sticks about half an inch wide. Rinse in cold water and place them on a towel to dry.

Deep-fry the potato sticks at about 320°F (160°C) (this is about when a piece of white bread becomes golden brown in 15 seconds) until they "sing" (4–8 minutes; they should not color too much). Pour them into a metal colander and shake lightly so that the fat runs off. Let cool for at least 15 minutes.

Deep-fry a second time, using the same fat from the first round, (not too many at once), at about 350°F (180°C) until they attain a nice golden color. Let the fat drain in a colander. Add salt and serve.

Note

I used to simply boil the potatoes in oil until they looked done, but my friend Per showed me this more exact method, which gives much better results.

Warning

Always have a large lid, fire blanket, and fire extinguisher close at hand when you're deep-frying.

Avoid frying over a gas burner! It only takes one drop of oil running down the side of the pot for the entire kitchen to light on fire, which happened to our neighbor the other year.

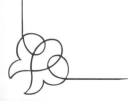

Edward Blom's gourmand burgers

These burgers are, as our friend Elisabet puts it, "supremely delicious, remarkably tall and quite spectacular," but also "trucker-who's-been-driving-all-night-gigantic." So perhaps they are not perfectly suited for children, when it comes to the size. Gunilla's youngest niece, Astrid, asked, rather aghast, "But why are they so big?" Our nieces also found it impossible to understand why we had filled them with a mountain of gross brown onions . . .
But most youngsters we know love our burgers,which are just as ideal for adults.
They are a take on my round beef patties (p. 124), which I created for the Swedish TV show *Breaking News with Filip & Fredrik*, in that instance served with a Brooklyn Lager.

——— 5 CHILD-SIZED BURGERS OR 3 ADUL-SIZED BURGERS ———

2 large onions

Tomato dressing

4 tbsp mayonnaise
3 tbsp tomato paste
1 tsp ketchup, optional

Mustard dressing

1½ tbsp Dijon mustard
4 tbsp mayonnaise (homemade or Hellman's)

Ground meat

1 lb (500 g) fresh ground beef of good quality
  (preferably a little coarse)
just over 1 tbsp Kikkoman soy sauce
2 tbsp Worcestershire sauce
4 hearty splashes of Tabasco
1 tsp black pepper, roughly crushed in a mortar
½–¾ tsp salt
1 large garlic clove, pressed
1 egg
butter and a fruity olive oil, and duck fat for
  frying

Per burger

1 roll of good quality (preferably coarse)
a few slices of cheese
1–2 slices of tomato
2 slices of bacon

Directions

Slice the onions into thin rings. Fry in butter over medium-high heat until they're brown and clump (as with Danish *hakkebøf*). Add salt when you start frying.
  Prepare the dressings.
  Combine the ingredients for the ground meat. Fry a sample to check that the ratio of spices and salt is right. Shape into 3–5 burgers (with wet or greased hands) and let them rest for a moment.
  Fry over high heat in olive oil mixed with butter.
  The burgers should have a raw center, but should be more fried than a grilled steak tartare. The surface should be dark brown.
  At the end, place a couple of slices of cheese on top of each burger and let it melt. Fry three slices of tomato and 2 bacon slices per burger. Cut the bread into three pieces so they look like the hamburger buns to the left. Fry them golden— preferably in duck fat.

Assembly

Spread tomato dressing on the bottom bread slice. Place the burger on top, with the cheese side up, bacon slices, and a slice of fried tomato.
  Add the middle bread slice. On that, place plenty of fried onion, and on top of that, add the mustard dressing.
  Place the lid on top.

Edward's standard stew

There's nothing I love more than stews, where a multitude of diverse ingredients slowly, slowly marry together into a rich, full-bodied, powerful flavor and texture.

Another good thing about stews is that they're perfect for cooking in bulk. But you have to remember that the stew runs the risk of sticking to the bottom. Make sure to have plenty of liquids at the start, which will be made to evaporate toward the end—to stir with a firm hand so as to prevent the stew from sticking to the bottom of the pot.

─────── APPROX. 40 NORMAL-SIZED PORTIONS ───────

13 lbs (6 kg) beef (chuck or fore shank)
  —any bones should cook along, but aren't counted as part of the weight
butter (lots required) and a neutral tasting oil
approx. 1 tbsp salt
a couple of bottles of cheap red wine
4½–6½ lbs (2–3 kg) onion
1 bulb of garlic
5½ lbs (2½ kg) root vegetables (rutabaga, parsnips, and possibly celeriac and Jerusalem artichokes)
1 lb (500 g) carrots
20 black peppercorns
2 tbsp dried thyme
1 bunch of fresh parsley
5 bay leaves
a couple of other herbs (tsp each of rosemary, basil, tarragon, herbes de province, etc—the more variety the richer the aroma)
1¼ cups (300 ml) Kikkoman soy sauce
5-7 marrow bones
assorted condiments available at home (see below)
a little concentrated ox stock (or broth)
a little concentrated vegetable stock (or broth)

Directions

Dice the meat into the size of large strawberries.

Chop the fat and sinews—nothing, absolutely nothing, is to be discarded. Brown the meat in an iron skillet with butter and oil over high heat so that it gets a dark color, and then toss it into a giant pot (5 gallon / 20 liters) or two 3-gallon (12 liter) ones. Use two frying pans. Don't fry too much meat at a time, otherwise the pan will get cold.

Salt the meat a little in each pan. Pour water or red wine into the pans after each batch to loosen whatever's been burned to the pan, and pour into the pot.

Peel, wash, and the cut all the vegetables into pieces the same size as the meat. Brown them over really high heat so they gain a lot of color (some pieces can even be allowed to burn a little). "Clean" the pans with water between batches and add the liquid to the pan.

Add the seasoning, soy, marrow bones, red wine, and as much water as needed to just cover the firm ingredients.

Simmer for a couple of hours. Stir every now and then, more often toward the end, so it doesn't stick to the bottom. When the pieces of meat become really tender, the root vegetables begin to crack a little, and the onion has "dissolved" completely, the stew is done.

Add salt to taste, and see if it needs any more flavoring (like stock wine, butter, currant juice, soy, balsamic vinegar, powdered dried mushroom, brandy, fish sauce, or more herbs and spices). Taste-testing is the most important and the most fun step, but may also be the most difficult; if you want to become a good amateur cook, you simply have to learn what is missing in the flavors of the dishes you make.

The stew can be eaten without accompaniments, but if it's meant to be enough for 40 people, it should be served with bread, couscous, bulgur, rice, or similar.

Note
You can add to the stew with meat and vegetables from the fridge and freezer, as long as they're finely chopped and boiled from the start.

If the stew is too runny, you can thicken it with a mixture of butter and flour.

Feast favorites

In the past twenty years, I've almost always celebrated
my birthday with around 30–50 guests. So, I have learned
what dishes work and don't work in those quantities.
Here are two of my classics.

Dijon chicken

This is the ultimate dish if you want to put something together for many people cheaply, quickly, and without much effort. An accomplished cook I knew from various club activities introduced me to this dish, but these are my proportions.

35-40 PORTIONS
---

13 lbs(6 kg) chicken breast, thawed and with all the juices drained (Avoid the discount chicken breasts that have that terrible spongy texture)

2 quarts (63 fl oz / 2 liters) crème fraiche (or sour cream)

3-3⅓ cups (700-800 ml) strong Dijon mustard

tarragon

black pepper

salt

butter or oil

Directions
Mix the crème fraiche and Dijon mustard.

If you like, season with a little tarragon and black pepper.

Grease two tall baking pans and distribute the breasts across them. Sprinkle with a little salt.

Pour the sauce on top and place the breasts in the oven (possibly covered with aluminum foil), at 350°F (175°C) until they are cooked through (about 1 hour). Preferably flip the chicken breasts after half the cooking time has passed.

For Serving
Served with rice, bulgur, couscous, quinoa, or something similar, plus bread if you have a large party.

Note
If you make a smaller serving size, you can cook it in a saucepan.

From archivist to TV personality

After a long day recording *Mellan skål och vägg* (*Between the Bowl and the Wall*) in Vadstena, we were treated to a gigantic brandy tasting. The photographer used the opportunity to take a photo that was then made available to download from TV8's website to use as a desktop wallpaper.

My TV career started in 2006 when *Finansnytt* (Swedish TV8's financial news show) wanted a little cultural history at the end of their broadcasts. The reporter Per Wikström traveled to Centrum för Näringslivshistoria (the Center for Business History in Stockholm), where he found me deep inside the archives. Thus, a collaboration was born that led to approximately ten documentaries about everything from the birth of mail order to thoughts on the perfect Swedish Christmas "julbord." When the program cancelled, I was given a miniseries on DI-TV: *Fredag med Edward* (*Friday with Edward*), where I talked about similar things live in the studio.

One day in 2008, I received a call from a journalist, Peter Andersson. He had worked at *Finansnytt* and seen the uncut segments. He thought I would be suitable for a history series he and photographer Björn Markusson were planning. I had to meet with him first before I realized this wasn't a practical joke a friend might be behind. We filmed a pilot episode, TV8 said yes, and suddenly I was a TV host!

Mellan skål och vägg (*Between the Bowl and the Wall*) *with Edward Blom* was a travel show about history: we visited castles, churches, forts, and ruins with happy 1920s jazz playing in the background. But we also ate sumptuous dinners and interviewed chefs in their kitchens. Somewhat unconventionally, many episodes would wrap up with us in an advanced stage of intoxication. Many still say that this is the best thing I've done.

Unfortunately, the channel and the production company didn't manage to agree about the terms for the planned second season, and so the show was sadly cancelled. When an acquaintance at another production company heard about it, he suggested a cooking show with my old idol, the ethnologist and gastronome Jan-Öjvind Swahn. This became *Edward Bloms gästabud* (*Edward Blom's Banquet*) in which I cooked food, visited breweries, milked goats, plucked geese, fished for eel, and baked *spettekaka*—all dressed in the same grey suit. The following year (2010), I was part of the judging panel on *Stjärnkockarna* (*Star Chefs*), a cooking show on TV3, where celebrities took their places at the stove. It was a great panel with top chefs, Melker Andersson, Tom Sjöstedt, and Lisa Förare Winbladh. The latter didn't just make sure to introduce me to half of Sweden's foodie population—she also brought me to many food industry events, such as Swedish Chef of the Year in 2010, where she connected me with Gunilla—so if it hadn't been for *Star Chefs*, I probably wouldn't be married!

Between the Bowl and the Wall
Edward Blom's Banquet
Stars Chefs
Menu
Hasselhoff—A Swedish talk show

That same summer, the chef, artist, and multitalented Ellen Wästfelt and I took over *Meny* (*Menu*) on Swedish radio which, to an avid radio listener such as myself, felt like a huge deal! We planned it thematically and gave the different episodes names such as "Grandma's food," "Love in a pot," and "Bellman's 18th century food."

So that no one would be able to complain they couldn't make these same dishes at home in their regular kitchen, we recorded everything in the producer's little summer cottage. Since then, I have had a multitude of TV appearances: a web show on cultural history called *Edward Blom's Stockholm* for the *Svenska Dagbladet;* weekly visits in *Breaking News with Filip and Fredrik* where I've mixed drinks, cooked food, and judged beverages and delicacies; *Halv åtta hos mig* (Swedish version of British *Come Dine With Me*); sabrage and more in *99 saker man ska göra innan man dör* (*99 things to do before you die*); guest at Aschberg's; guest expert at *Historieätarna* (History Eaters, Swedish *Supersizers*); "stand-up debut" in *Mitt liv är ett skämt* (*My Life is a Joke*); several visits to morning show couches, quiz shows, and debate shows—most often concerning food, drink, and cultural history in one combination or another.

It's the small, small details that do it

It started with conversations and dreams, long before we could afford to buy meat
and the wines we wanted to serve at our future dinner parties.
The correct cutlery, china, and the glassware for all the countless drinks were also missing. What
was right was defined by etiquette but also by our own tastes, which in Edward's case involved the
classical, bourgeois nineteenth-century ideal. But it all started with dreams, and he nurtured them.
I think we were about fifteen years old when Edward read aloud to me from an anthology of
literary meals—just one of many examples of how his interests cross pollinate.
The text was about a feast of juicy, whole roasted piglets and frothing tankards of ale.
Imagine that feast! So did Edward. However, it was not until several years later that he was able
to borrow or earn enough to realize his vision; the knowledge, commitment, and eccentric friends
were already there. Today, Edward's meals are getting close to the ideals of his youth.
With Gunilla, he has also found the perfect apartment setting, soaked in hundred-year-old
aesthetics, where the table is set with family china, silverware, and cold-pressed linen napkins. And
to top it all off, the food . . . Everything is, of course, prepared with the utmost chaos.
But when the dishes reach the dining hall, you only notice what's at their core: food that is
just as well made as it is well seasoned. Nevertheless, it's a small, trivial, and
nowadays almost forgotten detail that usually attracts the most attention.
Namely, that little doily that prevents the appetizer plate
from scratching the enamel on the main course plate.

Martin Melin, author and Edward's childhood friend

Variations on salmon loin
—gravlax, grilled, marinated

My wife, Gunilla, discovered the delicious salmon loin, a novelty of the Norwegian fishing industry, a couple years ago. It's unusually perfect for eating raw or half raw. We tried a couple of variations and settled on this combination platter of Swedish gravlax, Asian-inspired soy, and ginger-marinated salmon, as well as a grilled version with Italian pesto.

4 APPETIZER PORTIONS

14 oz (400 g) salmon loin

For the gravlax

1 tbsp sugar or the same amount of sweetener
1 tbsp salt
1½ tbsp dill
½ tsp crushed white pepper
gravlax sauce

For the marinated salmon

approx. ½ cup (100 ml) soy sauce
approx. 1 tbsp fresh ginger, grated
horseradish sauce (horseradish, mayonnaise, vinegar, whipping cream)

For the grilled salmon

salt
pepper
dill
olive oil
pesto

Directions

Quick Swedish gravlax

Cut out a piece of salmon of about 3½ oz (100 g) and rub it with pepper, salt, finely chopped dill, and sweetener. Place in a plastic bag and suck out the air. Let rest 3–5 hours in a fridge.

Dry the salmon. Cut into thin, diagonal slices. Serve with a dab of gravlax sauce (which you should preferably have whipped together yourself).

Asian marinated salmon

Dice about 3½ oz (100 g) of the salmon and place them in a marinade made of soy sauce and a little fresh grated ginger. Let sit 1–3 hours in the fridge.

Remove from the marinade and let the salmon drain. Serve with a dollop of horseradish sauce.

Horseradish sauce is easily made by stirring together 3½ tbsp (50 ml) finely grated horseradish, 1 tbsp cider vinegar, 2 tbsp mayonnaise, and 2 tbsp whipping cream (which is lightly whipped first).

Grilled salmon

Take about 7 oz (200 g) of salmon and cut into four portion-sized pieces.

Season them with salt, pepper, and a little dill, and rub with a high quality olive oil.

Fry them quickly in a very hot grill pan. The surface should brown a little, but the center should still be slightly raw. Serve with a large dab of tasty pesto.

Arrange these three varieties of salmon nicely on an appetizer plate with their toppings. A strong, dry German Riesling pairs perfectly, as does a wheat ale.

Winter warming soup

It was Gunilla's genius idea to take a traditional Jerusalem artichoke soup and add parsnips, of which we had plenty at home. It simplifies the dish, as parsnips are easier to peel than Jerusalem artichokes—but above all, it makes for a fantastic combination of flavors. The soup was part of the menu that Gunilla and I made for the food section of *Aftonbladet,* a Swedish paper. It makes an elegant appetizer as well as a cozy evening meal.

—— 4 APPETIZER PORTIONS, 2 AS A MAIN COURSE ——

$2/_3$ lb (300 g) Jerusalem artichokes
½ lb (200 g) parsnips
1–2 yellow onions
½ garlic clove, optional
duck fat or butter for frying
¾ cup (200 ml) dry white wine
1 $2/_3$ –2 cups (400–500 ml) vegetable broth
¾ cup (200 ml) whip cream
1–2 pinches of white pepper
about 1 tsp salt
a little concentrated vegetable stock, optional
½ tsp herbs (optional) try mixing a little of
  many different herbs
4–8 bacon slices
possibly a little smetana, crème fraiche, or
  sour cream

Directions

Peel and slice the onion, garlic, and root vegetables into pieces.

Fry the onion in a pot until soft (but not brown). Add the root vegetables toward the end, and the wine and broth a little after. Let simmer under cover until the root vegetables become really soft (about 25 minutes).

Mix the soup smooth with a hand mixer. Add the cream and bring to a boil.

Add pepper, salt, possibly a little concentrated stock and herbs to taste.

Serving

Serve with slices of very crispy bacon, which gives a lovely flavor contrast, possibly a dab of smetana, and a tasty bread. A dry sherry is a perfect complement.

Edward's Halv åtta dinner: chuck steak with roasted vegetables

I made this dish on *Halv åtta hos mig* (*Half Past Seven at My Place*; Swedish version of *Come Dine with Me*), and it won a shared first prize. The recipe was published in one of the cookbooks from the show and was nominated as "Helge's favorite." Since Helge Skoog, a popular Swedish actor, wasn't there during the recording, but was dubbed in afterward, we'd never actually met. But at the 2012 Gothenburg Book Fair, he walked right up to me, recognizing me as the "man with the fantastic prime rib."

——— 4 APPETIZER PORTIONS, 2 AS A MAIN COURSE ———

chuck steak

1 piece of chuck steak, approx. 2¼ lbs (1 kg)
butter for frying
1 carrot
a small piece of celeriac, optional
1½ onion
approx. 1 cup (200 ml) red wine
  (or 1 bottle of porter)
a small apple
1–2 garlic cloves
2 tsp Kikkoman soy sauce
at least 5 black peppercorns
a couple of juniper berries
a couple of allspice berries, optional
½–1 tsp salt
a handful of fresh lingonberries (or currants)
water

Roasted root vegetables

root vegetables (parsnips, rutabagas, carrots, and possibly Jerusalem artichokes)
red onion
oil and salt

Gravy ingredients, see p. 123

Directions

Brown the chuck steak on all sides in butter. Simmer it slowly with all the ingredients for the chuck steak—and as much water as needed to cover it all. Flip the chuck steak once while simmering. The meat is done when it's so tender you can pull it apart with a couple of spoons, which takes upward of 3½ hours.

While the chuck steak is simmering, peel and roughly chop the root vegetables and the onion into pieces as large as medium-sized strawberries. Take enough to cover a long baking pan with a thin layer of vegetables. Pour some neutral-flavored oil on top and sprinkle with coarse salt and roast in oven over high heat 15–20 minutes.

When the chuck steak is tender, divide it into large pieces with a pair of spoons and let it rest in the liquid for a while. Then, place it in aluminum foil, while the liquid reduces and the gravy is prepared according to the recipe on p. 123.

Serve the chuck steak on a large serving platter, with the roasted root vegetables and gravy and a bowl of jelly and some homemade pickled cucumber. If you want to butter up any guests who may think the food is too heavy, you can always prepare a green salad as well.

A strong red wine completes the meal.

Elisabet Melin, Lars Lundqvist, Annika Berg, Martin Melin, Edward Blom, and Gunilla Kinn Blom

Advice for a successful dinner party

1. Planning a menu

Take your time to ponder the menu. Think of it as a symphony, where one or possibly two dishes are the crescendos and the others make up the calmer movements. Try to adapt the meal to your guests, the time of year, what you personally want to get out of the evening, and what drinks you hope to serve. Avoid combining recipes that give more than 1¼ cups (300 ml) of cream per person, otherwise your guests will feel bloated and uncomfortable.

2. Time, talent, or money

Few are those who have time, money, *and* talent in the kitchen. But everyone has more of one than others, and that's enough. If you have all the time in the world, but empty coffers and aren't that used to the kitchen, fry smelt fish! If you're a skilled cook, but lack time or a decent budget, buy frozen fish and make a soufflé! If you have money, but neither the time nor much skill in the kitchen, open a can of foie gras and buy high-quality cheeses—everyone will revel in the meal. So consider what your particular strength might be!

3. Beautiful tables

As I write on p. 45, ugly food tastes better than beautiful food, but to create a festive feeling, you must put your efforts into every surrounding detail. Lustrous linen tablecloths and napkins, vintage tableware with lots of components, crystal carafes, and silver-plated cutlery are laughably inexpensive at auctions. Spend some time to iron the linens, polish the silver, and hand wash gilt-edged fine china, and your dinner party will be that much more splendid. Arranging flowers, folding napkins, making seasonal centerpieces, etc. are all bonuses, but are far from necessary. But candlelight can't be omitted. Turn off all the electric lighting and simply rely on candle-light. It creates a lovely feeling of romance—plus the silver can be unpolished and the food a dull gray brown and no one will notice!

4. Generosity

When the wine ran out at the wedding in Canaan, it was such a social catastrophe that Jesus performed the first miracle and transformed water into wine. Even today, this is your most important responsibility as a host: the wine (or beer) simply cannot run dry. A great wine is an amazing experience—but the only thing that's more important than the quality is the quantity. Start with a good wine (or beer), but always make sure to have something in reserve so there's enough to last through dinner. Unless the guests have been encouraged to pour for themselves (and really dare to do so), it's your duty as host to make sure no glass even approaches being empty. Let the wine become a symbolic reflection of you as a host!

5. Dare to be old fashioned!

Invitation cards with appointed dress code, cocktails with canapés—or a brännvinsbord, seating charts, speeches, sing-alongs, strict rules of inviting in return—and, not least, a large dose of courtesy from all parties have all evolved over generations of experience to avoid any discomfort and to promote pleasure. Don't be a radical iconoclast when it comes to dinners but instead follow—as Horace says—in the old master's footsteps.

Cheese tray

Every dinner party in the Blom home features a cheese tray. Many settle for three, four varieties
of a similar type of cheese (three hard cheeses or three bleu cheeses, for example).
Call me a gourmand, but I actually prefer twenty cheeses of all different kinds, (hard, soft-ripened, bleu,
washed rind, and finally an absolute wild card), as long as they're all of a very high quality.
Quality and quantity are equally important when it comes to cheese. I've solved any financial concerns
that may arise by simply buying the cheese from wholesalers, like in the photograph above, at Wijnjas in
Stockholm. For my part, I don't feel accompaniments are needed, as they only confuse the tastebuds—
possibly with the exception of thin, unsweetened rye crackers. But Gunilla appreciates biscuits, nuts, and
marmalades. Different wines suit different cheeses: sweet, botrytized wines with blue cheese, champagne
or red wine with cream cheeses, soft-ripened and hard cheeses, dry sherry with parmesan, etc.
If you want one wine to go with everything, a Madeira will work.

Madeira mousse

This is a variation of my Weincreme (p. 143), which is more in accordance with the traditional Swedish spirit and is one of my dessert favorites. Since Madeira tastes richer than white wine, you can use a smaller amount. That way you avoid the inconvenience of a roux. I think the mild yet elegant flavor is noble.

———————— AT LEAST 4 PORTIONS ————————

4 gelatin sheets
²/₃ cup (150 ml) sweet Madeira
3 eggs
1¼ cups (300 ml) whipping cream
   40%, room temperature
a couple of splashes of sugar substitute or
   4 tbsp (60 ml) sugar

Directions

Soak the gelatin sheets for 5 minutes. Heat the Madeira carefully in a pot and melt the gelatin in it.

Whip the cream until stiff peaks form. Separate the egg whites from the egg yolk, whisk the yolks lightly with the sweetener, then stir them into the cream.

Take ½ cup (100 ml) of the cream mixture and fold it into the Madeira–gelatin mixture. Then stir everything together. (The extra step reduces the risk of the gelatin solidifying into threads when it meets the cream.)

Sample to see if it is sweet enough. It should only be sweet enough to taste like a dessert.

Whisk the egg whites into a stiff foam with an electric mixer, and then carefully fold it in with large motions. Pour into a pretty bowl and let it stand in the refrigerator for a couple hours until it has set.

Serving

The result is most beautiful if you run warm water over the back of the bowl and tip the pudding out onto a serving plate, but it can also be presented in its bowl.

Appropriate toppings are grated, very dark chocolate—which gives a lovely flavor contrast—or a compote made of cherries and Madeira, if you want to accentuate the sweetness and fruitiness.

Quail Snerike
Cider-poached quail in Calvados sauce

In my shabby freshman dorm in Uppsala University, the average student's daily diet was abysmal. Some lived off Ramen noodles or spaghetti covered with ketchup. I bought cheap hens, prime rib, and root vegetables and made slowly cooked stews. Once, I found cheap frozen quail at the local supermarket. Since I often drank French cider and Calvados, this recipe came about organically in the hallway kitchen. How I enjoyed eating delicious fowl while the others were slurping noodles! The name is an homage to the best of fraternities—Snerike.

2 SMALL APPETIZERS OR LATE NIGHT PORTIONS

2 quails, plucked and washed
olive oil for frying
2 apples, wedged
6 small shallots, finely chopped
1 garlic clove, minced
salt, black pepper, and thyme (or
    "French herbs") to taste
dry, French cider, enough to cover (about 1 bottle)
butter, wheat flour, cream for the sauce
½ cognac glass Calvados

Directions

Brown the quails and a wedged apple in a cast-iron pot. Add half the shallot and garlic toward the end. Let it fry for a little while.

Add salt and season. Pour in enough cider to cover it all and simmer the quail over low heat until they're tender (about 45 minutes).

Meanwhile make a roux (step 1 in the gravy recipe on p. 123).

Place the quails in foil when they're done and reduce the liquid down to an appropriate concentration.

Fry the rest of the onions until they're soft.

Add the rest of the apple wedges toward the end.

Mix the liquid and whisk it into the roux, bring it to a boil, and simmer to the right consistency. When the sauce is done, add Calvados.

Serve the quails whole with the freshly fried onions and apple, the sauce, and even a parsnip purée. Both red wine and a strong French cider pair well.

Parsnip purée

Boil the parsnips until they're soft. Blend them, add a little cream, salt, and possibly a couple drops of truffle oil and butter.

Note

It's easier for the guests if you carve the quails and serve the meat. But I think that's a little mundane, as the whole point of serving small fowl is that luxurious feeling you get upon seeing a whole bird on your plate—otherwise you might as well have gone with one big bird.

Platon om konst
och skönhet

Institutionen för estetik
Uppsala universitet

Entrecôte Tegnér

A perfect dish for students who want to be thrifty, don't want to spend
the entire day in the kitchen, but still want a really gourmet meal. Even without an outdoor grill.
I often cooked this toward the end of my college days in my small kitchenette
on Tegnérgatan in Stockholm—hence the name.

──────── 4 LARGE PORTIONS ────────

1 large piece of whole entrecôte, at least
  2 lbs (900 g)—as marbled as possible
sea salt
large, dried red chili flakes
a little black pepper, optional
a little oil

Directions

Cut the entrecôte into four very thick slices. Lay
down the slices and hammer them out with your
fist so their surface gets wider and slightly thinner,
about ½ inch (1½ cm). Finish off by lightly tapping
the white fat deposites with the back of a chef's
knife; this breaks them up, which causes them to
melt more and provide more flavor.

Sprinkle with salt and chili and possibly a little
roughly ground black pepper. Rub the steaks with
a little oil.

Let them rest for an hour so they reach room
temperature.

Broil the meat quickly at the top of the oven
with the broiler turned on and the smoke alarm
turned off. Flip after half the time has elapsed.
They are tastiest when the meat is still red in the
middle but the surface is brown and has a few
stripes from the grate.

Serving

Served with garlic butter, homemade béarnaise sauce,
and grilled green asparagus and eggplant. Remember
that the side dishes take longer to prepare than the meat.

Cheese fondue

Fondue made from real Swiss Alp cheese and a good wine is one of the most
delicious things in the world. Cheese fondue made from inexpensive wine and
old edges of cheese is at least better than other options.
I loved throwing this fondue together during my university years, when my friends and I found ourselves
in my apartment with a case of the drunk munchies.

———— 2–4 PORTIONS, DEPENDING ON HOW FONDUE LOVING ONE IS ————

5½ cups (700 g) grated cheese, preferably a mixture
   of Appenzell, Gruyere, and Emmenthal
a small garlic clove
1²/₃ cups (400 ml) white wine
1 tbsp potato flour
1½ tbsp Kirschwasser (or in a pinch, another flavorful
   fruit brandy such as Grappa or Obstler)
seasoning: grated nutmeg, a splash of Tabasco,
   caraway, ground cumin, paprika (combine
   two or three of these to taste, not all in one go)

Directions

Rub the fondue pot (or saucepan, if that's all you
have) with the garlic clove. Save it.

Grate or slice the cheese. Pour most of the wine
into the fondue pot (but save 1 tbsp). Add the
cheese. Carefully melt over low heat.

Remove from the stove. Blend the potato flour
with the remaining wine and the brandy and add
to the fondue pot.

Stir while heating and let simmer until it
becomes an even, firm batter. Do not let it boil.

Add seasoning, and press in the rest of the
garlic clove you used to rub the pan with.

Serving

Serve in the fondue pot on a stand with a burner
underneath. Dip cubes of hearty whole-wheat
country bread, or for something different: cucumber, raw cauliflower, bell pepper, lightly fried
squash, or button mushrooms. Both white and red
wine pair well.

Three tips

1. A Swiss, Paco, taught me that when there's only a little fondue left in
the bottom of the pot, you can add an egg and stir it up. Then it becomes
scrambled egg and cheese, which you can dip the last pieces of bread
in it. It's also a perfect way to use any fondue leftovers for breakfast the
following morning.
2. In a Swedish Radio show with my colleague, Karsten Thurfjell,
I learned that old men from the Alps first dip their bread in Kirschwasser
and then in the fondue. Do become an old Alp man too!
3. If you base the fondue on inexpensive cheeses, you can flavor it with
chopped fresh chili and garlic.

OMSKRIVNING
Idé- och lärdomshistoria A:4 (även halvfart)
Tisdagen den 22 augusti 1995, kl. 17.00 - 21.00
Frågornas max.poäng anges inom parentes efter resp. fråga. Max. totalt:60

Var snäll och skriv TYDLIGT och KORTFATTAT!

LYCKA TILL!   Anders Lundgren, Franz Luttenberger och Mats Persson

1.   Vad innebar "Big Bang-teorin? (2 p.)

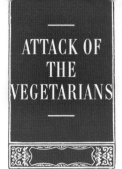

Spinach stew Mignon

Another dish I started to cook in my shabby kitchenette on Tegnérgatan, where I spent a large part of the nineties.

— ABOUT 2 SMALL PORTIONS AS A VEGETARIAN DISH, ALSO GOOD AS A SIDE DISH —

approx. 7 oz (200 g) leaf spinach (frozen works just fine, but weigh after it's been thawed and has drained; chopped spinach doesn't work at all)
approx. ½ cup (100 ml) olive oil
dried, red chili
1-2 garlic cloves
1-1½ oz (30-40 g) pine nuts
a little parmesan, optional
salt

Directions

Roast a handful of pine nuts in a dry cast-iron frying pan. They shouldn't blacken, just brown a little. Remove them.

Pour oil into the pan and let it heat up. Crumble in the chili and add the minced garlic.

Heat quickly in the oil, but don't let it get more than a tiny bit brown.

Add the spinach and cook until it is hot. Possibly add more olive oil if needed—the spinach should almost have a stew-like consistency. Season with salt to taste. Add pine nuts. Before serving, I would suggest you grate some parmesan on top.

Mashed rutabaga with cheddar

This is a dish I composed when my two oldest nieces came to dinner a few years back. Unfortunately, they happen to be vegetarians and hardly indulge in any alcohol, but other than that, they're wonderful people.

— 2 MAIN COURSE PORTIONS —

1 rutabaga (about 1 lb / 500 g)
salt
2 tbsp butter
black pepper
7 oz (200 g) cheddar

Directions

Peel and cut a rutabaga into a couple of pieces and simmer them in salted water until soft (20–30 minutes).

Mash with a potato masher. Bring to a boil.

Add butter and plenty of black pepper, freshly ground or crushed in a mortar and pestle, and add salt to taste.

Chop the cheddar into large pieces and stir it into the mash.

Remove from the heat and let stand a minute so the cheese begins to melt, but it shouldn't dissolve completely.

Serve immediately!

Pasta Fanucci

My friend Mats taught me how to make this Italian dish in my dirty and microscopic kitchenette on Tegnérgatan sometime during the nineties, when we invited two ladies for dinner. The evening ended with a waltz—despite the fact that the room itself was only 150 square feet.

— 4 PORTIONS —

1 lb (500 g) broccoli (preferably fresh)
a small, very strong, dried red chili
   (preferably peperoncino intero), crushed
2 garlic cloves
2/3 cup (150 ml) high-quality olive oil
salt

Directions

Cook the broccoli with the chili and 1 tsp salt, until it is slightly softer than it would be if it were to be eaten as is. Drain. Crush the garlic and add it in. Pour in the olive oil.

Mash with a potato masher or run quickly in a blender. If needed, dilute with a little of the water from boiling the broccoli.

Add salt to taste (about ½ tsp), but not too little.

Serving

Serve as a pasta sauce, with gnocchi or tagliatelle, for example, and grate a little fresh parmesan on top. This is also a very nice accompaniment to meat or fish, but in that case, use less oil.

Note

Mats and another Italy enthusiast from our university days tried to convince the rest of us that "Fanucci!" was the most exuberant way to toast in Italian. In reality, it's a surname. In honor of those days, the pasta sauce will be named thus.

Edward's vegetarian "meat soup"

A wonderfully hearty vegetable soup that goes down superb on a brisk autumn day.
All the cream makes the soup filling, the green pepper gives it zing and, thanks to the fried onion
and soy sauce, it has a hint of meat about its taste. This one is, of course,
also composed in honor of my vegetarian nieces.

————— 6 PORTIONS AS A MAIN COURSE —————

¾–1 lb (400–500 g) Brussels sprouts
7–10 oz (200–300 g) green beans
½ cup (100 ml) Kikkoman soy sauce
½ tsp salt
½–1 tsp rosemary
1 tbsp dried green pepper
1 tbsp fresh parsley
½ tsp each of oregano and basil,
   and even some additional herbs
   for a more complex flavor
3 large yellow onions, sliced
2–3 garlic cloves, minced
10 oz (300 g) squash, chopped
1 carrot, sliced
1 can of peas and carrots, optional
3–3½ cups (700–800 ml) whipping cream
¼ cup (50 ml) white wine, optional
a splash of Madeira, a little honey, or jelly,
optional
butter and olive oil

Directions

Fill a large cast-iron pot or saucepan halfway
with brussel sprouts and green beans and
about 1 cup of water. Add the soy sauce,
salt, and the herbs and bring to a boil.

Fry the onions in butter over high heat in a
cast-iron skillet. Let them get really brown, so
much so that some of the smaller pieces even
burn a little.

Add the garlic toward the end and let it
fry for a moment.

Add the onion to the boiling vegetables.

Swirl a cup of water around the skillet to loosen any leftover flavor and pour into the soup.

Fry the squash and carrot in olive oil.

Pour into the pot. Simmer over low heat until
the vegetables become really soft (about 15 minutes). If you like, add carrots and peas.

Blend in a blender until smooth. Add cream and
wine if you choose.

Bring the soup to a boil. Then simmer over low
heat for 15 minutes while stirring from time to
time—at this point, the soup has a splash zone of
about a yard, so be careful.

If you like, add something sweet and fruity to
taste (especially if you didn't use carrots), such
as a little Madeira, currant jelly, apple juice, or a
spoonful of honey.

Note

Some of the squash can be finely chopped and added in after the immersion blender has been run, if you would prefer a somewhat more
beautiful soup dotted with little green pieces. (My youngest niece strongly objects to this, however.)

More vegetarian dishes:
Mexican cheese and chili soup p. 20
Hummus with hazelnuts p. 174
Jaz's rice p. 113
Cheese fondue p. 101
Winter warming soup p. 89
Welsh rarebite p. 135
Rum Punch p. 185

Good things to have at home

Soy sauce—a dash heightens the flavor of most things.

Lemons—Kennst du das Land? Buy organic, and you can use the zest just as much as the juice without getting poisoned.

Coffee—you can cook without ever opening a bottle of wine, but seldom without a cup of coffee.

Porter—"Sub luna bibo. Dark is my ale, black-malted grain its heart," wrote Karlfeldt and I, too, enjoy porter beneath the crescent moon.

Tabasco—happiness in a little bottle.

Worcestershire sauce—has a special place in my heart. Can save anything that's missing that certain something.

Red wine—just as much in Edward as in the pot.

St. Lawrence with the broiler is the patron saint of cooks and chefs and therefore has a given place in every kitchen. Also responsible for archivists.

Champagne—you never know when you suddenly have a reason to celebrate.

Foie gras—nothing else satisfies the taste buds as intensely.

Cookbook—I cook food by feel, but I also use cookbooks to evolve. This is my first one.

Butter—needed for just about everything and can never be replaced with margarine.

Walnuts—a staple in our home: in yogurt, roasted in salad, in pesto and dips, in desserts and confections, and as a snack. Tasty and healthy.

Spices—life would be poorer without them! Have a well-stocked spice rack, fresh herbs growing on the windowsill, and big bags of dill and parsley in the freezer.

Swedish anchovy fillets (sprats)—always have a can in the fridge so you can throw together a gentleman's delight, nighttime sandwiches, or another improvised snack that pairs with ale and spirits.

Mustard—you must always have a couple of varieties at home. I prefer the sugar-free ones.

Lingonberries—one of my passions. We keep large bags in the freezer and a bowl of thawed ones in the fridge. Keeps for weeks without sugar. Delicious in most things.

Olive oil—flavoring, frying pan assistant and consistency giver; do as the Spaniards do and drown your food in it—and make sure to have several varieties at home.

Västerbotten cheese—Sweden's gift to mankind. When at its best (the quality can vary) it beats every other hard cheese.

Duck fat—ten years ago I was foolish enough to believe a person could live without this, but I was wrong.

Eggs—our most affordable animal-derived foodstuff.

Cream—a couple of spoonfuls in everything makes life prettier..

Onion and garlic—spices, as well as staples. No one with a sack of onions will go wanting.

Bacon—because it exists!

GREBBESTADS
ANSJOVIS
ORIGINAL
Abba

Graisse de Canard
Poids net : 600 G.

Inter-rail dinner

I've eaten variations of this meal in innumerable train compartments
as the landscape flew past outside the window or as I sat under the blazing sun on a luggage trolley
on a country platform while changing trains—with a newspaper
for a tablecloth. But you can also eat an "inter-rail dinner" at home—it's my favorite on days
when I return home late and am too tired to cook, or I just don't feel like having a hot meal.
The exact components can vary, but you should have a really good salami
or air-dried meat, at least one really high-quality cheese, walnuts or olives, and half
a bottle of simple red wine. To get the right inter-rail feel, you shouldn't buy
ready-sliced charcuterie, but instead get a chunk of it and cut it with a small penknife.
A simple and quick meal that is still substantial, genuine, and healthy!
It can all be expanded into a "luxury inter-rail dinner," with all sorts of components that can
be purchased at a charming hole in the wall somewhere along the European railway network,
such as: freshly baked bread, paté or goose liver, a can of rillettes, a couple figs,
a sun-kissed peach, a whole bottle of château wine, some pickled
vegetables, and a cigar.

Jaz's chicken curry

My friend Jaz (Jasvinder) cooked this delightful dish many times during my school year in Trier from 1989 to 1990. I'd never eaten Indian food before, and I was completely enchanted! Even though I've enjoyed good Indian food since then, I still find this to be one of the most delicious Indian dishes I've ever eaten. In its original form, without chili, it's not in the least bit hot, but very mellow and aromatic. The butter oil and masala spice form the soul of this dish. For a long time, Jaz mailed me her mother's own masala mix from England, but these days I have to make do with garam masala from the store.

3-4 PORTIONS

1 very large chicken (or even better, a young rooster)
¾ cup (200 ml) ghee (can be prepared with butter, see next page)
1-2 tsp whole cumin
6 large onions
1 tbsp salt
2-3 large garlic cloves, chopped
1 heaping tbsp grated, fresh ginger
a little fresh chili, optional (delicious if you like it spicy, but it can easily take away a little from the other flavors)
1 tbsp masala (if you don't have Jaz's homemade mix, you can use garam masala from an Indian store, in which case I think you should use 2 tbsp)
1 tbsp turmeric
½-1 can of chopped tomatoes (Jaz claims to use a whole can nowadays, but I'm positive she only used half twenty years ago)
chopped, fresh cilantro

Directions

Carve the chicken anatomically (legs, breast pieces, and wings) and fry the parts in ghee.

Heat just over ⅔ cup (150 ml) ghee in a large pot. If you use too little ghee, it'll burn and stick and the consistency of the sauce may be all wrong, so if you're afraid of fat you might as well not bother with this dish.

Add cumin and onions cut into eight wedges each. Add salt and stir. Cover with a lid and let the onions simmer over very low heat. Stir every so often. They must not brown. After simmering for 20 minutes, see if the onions are really soft, and if so, add ginger, garlic, and possibly a little chili and stir. Cover and continue to simmer for 10 minutes while stirring regularly.

Add masala and turmeric and stir. Simmer another 5 minutes.

Add the chicken and stir. Cover with the lid Simmer for another 30 minutes or so, until the chicken is completely cooked through and the onion has almost dissolved.

Stir every 5–10 minutes. Finally, add fresh, finely chopped cilantro.

Served with basmati rice and naan (see next page).

Note
Jaz says that you can also make lamb curry with the same recipe, but you'll have to simmer the curry for 45–60 minutes instead of 30 minutes.

Rice on the Side

Jaz usually serves this rice with the curry; it also pairs well with a cooked vegetable as a vegetarian option.

200–250 g Indian basmati rice of the highest quality
water
1 large onion
ghee
just over 1 tsp cumin
½–1 tsp salt
just over ¼ tsp masala

Directions

Rinse the rice a couple times and let it soak in cold water for 30 minutes.

Slice the onion and lightly fry it in plenty of ghee. Add cumin, salt, and masala. Fry for about 5 minutes until the onion is translucent.

Drain the rice and then add it to the pot with the onion. Add twice as much water as rice.

Cover with a lid, bring to a boil, and then simmer over low heat for about 20 minutes. Stir the rice halfway through the cooking time. Check occasionally that the rice isn't sticking. Dilute with hot water if it gets too dry.

How to make ghee (Indian butter oil)

Ghee is a sort of refined butter and it is available in Indian grocery stores. It is, however, quite easy to make yourself: simmer five sticks of butter for at least an hour (keep checking on it so it doesn't catch fire). Let it cool.

Skim and strain away the deposit at the bottom.

Shrimp sandwich

–all delicious and just too much!

A dish, at least in Sweden, associated with traveling is the shrimp sandwich. Originally, most likely inspired by a Danish "*æg med rejersmørrebrød*," it was linked to voyages across the Øresund and the Kattegat, but it has since come to be eaten at airports, cafes, and on trains. Therefore, a couple years ago, I got to make a short film about the sandwich for the aviation department in honor of Shrimp Sandwich Day on the 14th of October. In small-town Sweden, where no one dared to whisper of things such as goose liver or oysters, the shrimp sandwich was the closest to *la dolce vita* one could get. Even though it's fairly ordinary, there's something Baroque and excessive about it.

In the short film, I spontaneously happened to let out: "It's mayonaaaaise, and it's shrimp, and it's all delicious and it's just too much!" In the original Swedsih, this statement sounded so lyrical that someone recorded it and put together a remix that became a YouTube sensation. That's how "Allting gott och alldeles för mycket" became something of a motto for me, first as a slogan on my homepage and then as the original Swedish title of this book.

An authentic shrimp sandwich is fantastic and it's a perfect example of a dish that's often more expensive to make at home than to order in the pub. But finding the perfect shrimp sandwich is not easy. Since it is born out of the Danish *smørrebrød*— the open-faced sandwich—it's important to follow the smørrebrød principle of bread, a main

ingredient, at least one secondary ingredient, and sauce. To claim a shrimp sandwich only consists of shrimp and bread is nonsense, but the shrimp also shouldn't be drenched beneath a mound of strange garnishes, such as vegetables—or as I, sadly, experienced recently at an otherwise excellent restaurant in Stockholm: roasted onion!

The most important thing is that it's made from fresh, deep-water shrimp, and there should be "shrimp in congestion," meaning lots of shrimp packed tightly together. Almost just as important is that they rest on a mountain of homemade mayonnaise. To qualify as a "sandwich," there also has to be bread; of course, it shouldn't be just any sweet, spongy bread, but rather quite a rustic, high-quality bread. And on to the secondary ingredient—a sliced hardboiled egg—which cannot overshadow the rest, but should simply be there for support.

Finally a small wedge of lemon is acceptable, as well as a sprig of dill and, possibly, a small lettuce leaf—provided that it's not iceberg lettuce. Nothing else should ever be added—but it's completely acceptable to drink Pink Gin Soda, white wine, beer, snaps, or even a glass of champagne with the shrimp sandwich.

Pepper shellfish like in Singapore

When I was in Singapore on my way to an international
conference on archives, I was served a wonderful pepper crab—
a splendid way to cook shellfish, particularly if you love butter.

Directions

Place two sticks of butter in a large pot. Add plenty of crushed garlic, some grated ginger, salt, and
plenty of roughly crushed black pepper (the pepper will give the dish its character). Throw in assorted
shellfish, preferably raw. Splash in a little oyster sauce (and preferably some Chinese rice wine).
Fry the shellfish until they're done. (Larger, raw shellfish, such as whole crab, should be
simmered while covered, in which case you should add slightly more liquid.)
I've made this dish with shrimp, scallops, lobster, and crab.
Don't hesitate to use different kinds of shellfish!

Mobile-style oysters

For many years, I would turn up my nose if someone so much as splashed a little vinaigrette on their oysters. Oysters were to be eaten unseasoned—and of course raw. Variations in which oysters were placed in an oven and drenched in sauce were nothing short of barbaric. But . . . after Gunilla (who was a foreign correspondent in New York for eleven years) got me to live in the United States part time for a year, I was floored. The classic Oysters Rockefeller from the Grand Central Oyster Bar were something undeniably special. And when we ended up in the South for a couple days, any remaining resistance was completely blown away. The breaded oysters we ate at Wintzell's Oyster House in Mobile, Alabama, made me cry tears of joy. The ones at Arnaud's in New Orleans were just as good—but more expensive. Here is my interpretation, but I do what I recently learned in Vietnam and let the center remain slightly raw. —Admittedly, with the price of oysters these days, it would be an atrocity to stick them in the oven. But perhaps you could treat yourself on New Year's Eve, your anniversary, or some other very special event.

— 4 SMALL PORTIONS, 6 OYSTERS EACH —

24 oysters

For sauces and toppings, see below.

Directions
Prepare all the sauces as described below.

Rinse the oysters, open them, and place them in a baking pan that has first been covered with coarse salt (to make them stand up straight).

Add the sauces according to each recipe.

Broil (with the oven's broiler setting) quite high up in the oven for 3–5 minutes. They should attain a nice color on the surface, but still be a little creamy in the middle. (If you like, prepare an extra oyster so you can sample the taste before the entire batch heads out to the dinner table.)

Serve smoking hot!

Cheese, chili, and bacon oysters
3¼ oz (90 g) bacon
1-2 jalapenos
½ garlic clove
1 tsp shallot
3½-4½ oz (100-125 g) cheddar, grated
just over 2 tbsp Philadelphia cream cheese
a splash of hickory liquid smoke

Directions
Fry the bacon until very crispy. Remove the slices and let them drain. Crush them into fine pieces with a pestle.

Remove the seeds and chop the jalapeno finely. Chop all the onion finely. Fry it in oil until light brown and add the jalapeno toward the end.

Grate the cheese. Stir all the ingredients together.

Season with the liquid smoke.

Dollop as much of the paste as you can (about 1½ tbsp) over a third of the oysters.

To be continued on next page

How to open oysters!

Wear gloves to protect your hands. Stick the tip of
the oyster knife into the closed opening at the tip of the oyster.
Wiggle the knife back and forth, and up and down, and at the same
time, press carefully inward. When the oyster opens up, bring
the knife around the whole oyster. Finally, cut the gelatinous
oyster body from its muscle on the detached "lid."
Be careful not to cut yourself, and don't break the tip of the knife
inside the oyster lest you or a guest accidentally swallow it
—which happened once at my place.

Oysters Rockefeller à la Grand Central Station

Create a Hollandaise sauce as on p. 152, but use a little more salt and a couple generous splashes of Tabasco instead of saffron.

Spinach sauce

5⅓ oz (150 g) leaf spinach
approx. ¼ tsp salt
butter
⅓ garlic clove, finely chopped
1 small shallot, finely chopped
approx. ⅔ tbsp wheat flour
approx. ¼ cup (50 ml) whipping cream
approx. 2 tbsp (30 ml) dry white wine
a little bit of ground black pepper and ground
nutmeg to taste

Directions

Cook the spinach 2–3 minutes in salted water. Remove and let drain. Run in a salad spinner or squeeze dry with a towel. Chop.

Melt the butter and fry the garlic and shallot until it is soft but not brown (about 5 minutes). Add the spinach and fry for a moment while stirring.

Make a fairly thick sauce from butter, flour, cream, and white wine (see p. 169 & 171). Stir in spinach, shallot, and garlic and let it simmer a little. Season with salt and spices to taste.

Add just about a tablespoon of the spinach sauce each onto a third of the oysters.

After 1½ minutes in the oven, dab on just about a tablespoon of Hollandaise.

Oysters Bienville

¼ large garlic clove
1¾ tbsp (25 ml) chopped green onion
2 small mushrooms (Button mushrooms)
butter
¾ tbsp wheat flour
¼ cup (50 ml) fish or chicken stock (or broth)
⅔ cup (150 ml) cream
1 small egg yolk
¼ cup (50 ml) dry white wine
5 shrimp
approx. ⅓ cup (150 ml) crab meat
some cut parsley
some herbs
a pinch of cayenne pepper
a splash of Tabasco
salt and pepper
half a pinch of paprika powder
a splash of shellfish stock, optional
a little brandy
breadcrumbs
Parmesan cheese

Directions

Finely chop the garlic, the green onions, and mushrooms. Fry them in little butter until soft, but don't let them brown. Add a little salt and stir in the flour. Add the stock and let it simmer for 15 minutes.

Whisk together the cream and egg yolk. Remove the sauce from the heat and pour in first the egg mixture and then the wine while stirring vigorously. (The consistency should be something between a sauce and stew.)

Chop the shrimp and add them and the crab meat.

Add all the other spices and herbs to taste, and possibly some shellfish stock, more salt, and why not a little brandy?

Simmer carefully for a couple minutes while stirring, but don't let it boil.

Top a third of the oysters each with about 1 tbsp of the sauce. Sprinkle a little breadcrumbs and grate a plentiful layer of Parmesan on top.

Note
The three oyster sauces also work perfectly for making green clams au gratin.

Uncle Edward's poached salmon

I can't remember ever having poached salmon as a child.
Warm smoked, cold smoked, salmon pudding, salmon cutlet, yes—but never poached.
When I was about twenty-five, my grandmother invited me to a spring dinner where she served
poached salmon and I was all but possessed by both its flavor and texture.
Of all the delicious things one can do with salmon, this is, to my thinking (and second to gravlax),
the foremost. Because of my admiration, my grandma made poached salmon on many more occasions.
I have increased her traditional seasoning a little and reduced the inner temperature slightly.

A large piece of salmon with the bones and skin remaining, calculate ½ lb (250 g) salmon per person

For every liter of poaching liquid

4¼ cups (1 liter) water
1½ tbsp chopped dill (frozen is fine)
¼ tsp dill seeds, optional
8 white peppercorns
4-7 allspice berries
1 tbsp salt
1 tbsp vinegar

Directions

Boil all the ingredients for the poaching liquid for 10 minutes, just without the fish (2 quarts–1 gallon [2–4 liters] of poaching liquid will be needed, depending on the size of the fish and the pot).

Lay the salmon in the liquid and simmer carefully while covered 25–70 minutes (depending on the thickness of the fish).

When it attains an inner temperature of 130°F (55°C) (you can pull the meat from the bone and see if a tiny, tiny raw center remains) remove the pot from the heat and cool it quickly in a water bath. Let stand for about 24 hours in its poaching liquid.

Remove the fish, remove the skin, and serve beautiful pieces at the table.

Serving

Poached salmon should be served with boiled green vegetables and homemade mayonnaise. A friend who found this dish "moss-covered and out-dated" nevertheless recommended a sour cream-based sauce and mayonnaise flavored with dill, Dijon mustard, capers, and lemon zest to bring it into the twenty-first century.

Note

The larger the salmon is, the tastier it becomes when poached. In other words, it's better to buy a giant salmon than a small one.

Are you going to make poached salmon for so many people that it seems unreasonable? In that case, it's best to place portion-sized pieces in baking pans and pour the boiling poaching liquid on top—that way they will cook as they're cooling.

Warning!

If you use wild salmon, the fish must be frozen for three days or must reach an internal temperature of at least 140°F (60°C).

Meat stock:

You can make the best stock from the liquid leftover after pan-searing or boiling meat. Or you can use stock made special for the purpose from bones and vegetables. Beef and game give more flavor than pork. If you roast meat in the oven, you should pour a little water in the baking pan to catch the drippings.

The least flavorful version can be achieved after hastily searing a piece of meat in the frying pan but even that little is worth reducing with a cup of water.

Superb gravy

Brown gravy doesn't sound fun, and it can be the most depressing thing in the world if it's made from powdered mixes. But done right, it can also be one of life's greater delights! My grandmother taught me how to make gravy when I was very young, and my education lasted for decades before I finally managed to surpass the master. It was grandma who asked me to take care of the gravy at each meal. Gravy is suitable for all kinds of meat, and you always reserve the right to mash it into your potatoes at the dinner table—even if etiquette forbids it. Because gastronomy comes before social etiquette! You may even eat it with a regular spoon (if you don't have a sauce spoon on hand), which is what food historian Jan-Öjvind Swahn did with my rook sauce when we recorded the TV series *Edward Blom's Banquet*. I've rarely felt more honored. He did not, however, call it brown gravy— but rather Sauce Espagnole, because it sounded better, but strictly speaking, it should contain a spoonful of tomato paste to be considered Sauce Espagnole. A gravy is never better than its base. The stronger the flavor of meat, onion, and vegetables, etc. that are brought out by the cream and are complemented with spices, the better the gravy becomes.

4 PORTIONS

3½–7 tbsp (50-100 g) butter
½ cup (100 ml) wheat flour
1⅓ cups (400 ml) whipping cream
approx. 3 cup (700 ml) flavorful meat stock, see inset!
a little potato or vegetable broth, optional

Directions
Roux: Melt the butter and let it brown a little. Stir in the wheat flour and let it bubble for a minute while stirring constantly (to remove the flour taste), without it turning brown. Reduce the temperature and let it simmer for a short moment, until it smells faintly of hazelnut.

Add the cream (preferably heated) a little at a time while stirring constantly until it becomes a thick stew. Let the roux stand and swell until the meat is ready.

If the gravy is runny, reduce (boil down) it until it has a strong and delicious flavor (while keeping the meat warm).

Add meat stock in batches to the roux, until the gravy is thick enough. If you've boiled carrots, onions, prunes, or the like together with the meat, add them to the gravy and blend until smooth with an immersion blender. This adds a lot of flavor. If the sauce is too thick and you've used up all the meat stock, dilute with vegetable or potato broth. Let it simmer for at least ten minutes.

Sampling
Start with the meat flavor—if the meat stock wasn't strong enough, it'll have to be intensified with concentrated beef stock. If it's too strong, dilute with more cream. All gravies also need some quality Japanese soy sauce to become more full-bodied. If you want the gravy to have a browner color, you can also add a little caramel coloring.

Often you need a little fruity sweetness in the form of jelly, juice, or fortified wine. Other than that, you'll just have to taste it to see if anything is missing: Sweetness? Saltiness? Roundness? Strength? Try to find the perfect balance with soy sauce, salt, currant juice, rowanberry jelly, lingonberry jam, fortified wine, pepper, or herbs.

Preferably finish by binding with a pat of butter. When tasting, the gravy should be almost too intense in flavor for it to go perfectly with the meat and the vegetables. In extreme cases, you may have to use the juice from Swedish anchovy fillets or skarpsill, Worcestershire sauce, or brandy. You can vary the flavor with chopped marrow, mushrooms, or tomato.

Edward Blom's ground beef patties

This is a ridiculously simple and inexpensive dish that still offers a magnificent flavor experience—but everything will be ruined if you cook the patties through completely or if you don't have enough mayonnaise.

— 4 GIANT PORTIONS —

Ground beef mixture

2¼ lbs (1 kg) ground beef (preferably coarsely ground)
2¼ tbsp Kikkoman soy sauce
⅓ cup (75 ml) Worcestershire sauce
4-5 generous dashes of Tabasco
2-3 garlic cloves, pressed
1½ tsp salt
2 eggs
2 tsp black pepper, coarsely crushed in mortar
butter, olive oil for frying

Accompaniments

8 onions
Dijon mustard
mayonnaise (mild, preferably homemade, otherwise Hellman's)
tomato paste

Directions

Slice the onions into thin rings. Fry in butter over low heat until they're brown and clump together in a mass, as they would when accompanying steak and onions (20–30 minutes). Add salt when you start frying.

Combine all the ingredients for the meat mixture and work with the paste for a minute at most. Fry up a sample and taste; you'll possibly need to add more salt. Form into medium-sized patties (with wet or oiled hands) and let them rest a moment.

Fry in olive oil mixed with butter over high heat. The patties should have a raw center, but be more fried than broiled steak tartare. The surface should be dark brown.

Serving

Serve with a mountain of fried onion and large dollops of Dijon mustard, mayonnaise, and tomato paste. Alternate between bites of beef patty, mayonnaise, onion, and Dijon, and bites of beef patty, mayonnaise, and tomato paste, which allows for different taste experiences.

If you want side dishes, I'd recommend a slice of bread, fried potatoes, or some sort of vegetable. Porter, British ale, water, or red wine go perfectly with this.

Lamb stew

There's no particular story behind this dish, but since stew
is the type of food I like most, I figured the book could use another recipe.
It also substantiates the theory that the more boring a dish looks, the tastier it is!

3⅓ lbs (1.5 kg) lamb brisket with bone
olive oil and butter for frying
5 yellow onions
2 garlic cloves
approx. 1 lb (500 g) fennel and spring cabbage (or
    other suitable vegetables)
½–¾ cup (100–200 ml) canned cherry tomatoes
2 bay leaves
1 bunch of parsley
approx. 1 tsp Herbes de Provence or French herbs
½–1 tsp sage
preferably 2–3 tsp dried mint (or 1 tsp fresh)
1½ tsp savory
1 tsp whole, dried coriander
1 heaping tsp whole black pepper
approx. 1–2 tsp salt
1 tbsp Kikkoman soy sauce
1 tbsp concentrated vegetable stock
½ cup (100 ml) whipping cream 40%
a couple dashes Worcestershire sauce
olive oil and butter

Directions

Cut the brisket into large pieces and fry them in butter.

Fry the onions and garlic in olive oil. Add vegetables, spices, salt, soy sauce, stock, and enough water to cover two thirds of the meat.

Simmer for 2½–4 hours until all the meat has fallen off the bone and the fat has melted. Stir every now and then, and dilute with more water if it becomes too dry.

Add the cream toward the end, and remove the bones that have been boiled clean and the tough membranes if you have squeamish guests.

If the stew is too runny, uncover and simmer while stirring until it attains a proper stew-like consistency—but be careful it doesn't burn.

Taste and add a couple of dashes of Worcestershire sauce and a few other spices, if needed.

Cheese spread

This spread, called potkäs, is a fantastic way to transform hardened odds and ends of leftover cheese and shabby over-ripe bleu cheese into something really delicious. It's very good with herring, as well as on the cheese tray, and it's optimal to keep in the fridge if you're one of those Winnie the Pooh–types, who get sudden cravings to "have a smackerel" of something.

Directions

Grate an assorted variety of hard cheeses. Dry cheese rinds are perfect, but take care to remove the wax edges. If you like, add a little dessert cheese, especially Bleu, soft-ripened, and washed rind cheese, and use the edges from these as well. (If they're unpasteurized, all sorts of flavors can develop.)

Mash the cheese with room temperature butter (about half as much butter as you have cheese).

Add a snaps glass of brandy, brännvin, or whiskey. Season with cumin and a little ground nutmeg, and stir into a smooth cream. Store the cheese spread in a cool place, ideally in a stoneware pot, and fill it up with new cheese as more leftovers come along.

Bring out the cheese spread with ample time before it is to be eaten so it can be enjoyed at room temperature—usually on crispbread. But I'm happy to eat it with a spoon.

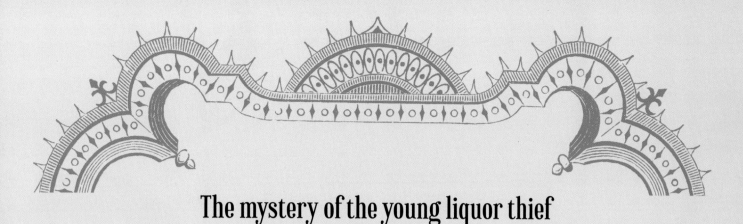

The mystery of the young liquor thief

In music, they speak of people with perfect pitch. I believe skilled chefs and gourmands have that kind of ability when it comes to the palate. I've cooked many dishes according to Edward's recipes or those of other people who make fantastic food. It usually turns out very delicious, but is seldom as delicious as the original. There's some kind of non-verbal knowledge in sampling, for example, a soup and then knowing exactly what spices or ingredients are missing and in what amount. As early as age thirteen, Edward had this ability, and he put it to use making delectable soups, meat dishes, and sauces for the family.

But it was less enjoyable when I discovered that a certain young family member hadn't just developed a weakness for cooking—but also for his parents' liquor cabinet, which was stored on a high shelf in the pantry. That type of "gourmet enjoyment," being out with inebriated friends, was not something we wanted for him. The expensive bottle of brandy (a fortieth birthday gift) had clearly diminished, as had the Madeira and sherry.

The only possible thief was Edward. His sister wrinkled her nose at strong liquor, and neither my wife, Ninnie, nor I had the habit of sneaking a drink in secret. Of course, we were disappointed. Edward had never stolen anything before. Our first thought was to confront him immediately. But then we thought that maybe we should approach the problem a little more psychologically and consider who might be the new, unsuitable friends he had fallen in with. So we waited.

A couple days later, it was Saturday and the family gathered together. Edward cooked the veal steak, his sister Anna set the table, Ninnie chopped lettuce, and I peeled the potatoes. It was going to be a hearty Saturday dinner and soon Edward was whisking the sauce. Suddenly I hear a glugging sound and see a hefty dose of the above-mentioned, very fine, and very expensive brandy disappear into the sauce. Edward closes the bottle—and in the next second it's back in its place above the pantry, and Edward samples the sauce with a look of satisfaction.

It's no wonder the sauces tasted so phenomenal, and it's no wonder my wife and I were both so overjoyed and relieved to solve the mystery of the young liquor thief.

James Blom, Edward's father

BEER IN FOOD

Porter steak

Porter is one of the finest flavors that can waltz across one's taste buds.
Porter steak is a genuine classic. I usually keep myself entertained by drinking porter while
I'm making the steak, and with the finished product—but in this case, it should be an imperial stout.

―――――――――― 4–5 PORTIONS ――――――――――

1 beef steak, approx. 2¼ lbs (1 kg) (of loin,
   topside or fore shank)
a little butter and oil
2–3 garlic cloves, sliced
2 onions, wedged
½ cup (100 ml) Kikkoman soy sauce
½ cup (100 ml) concentrated blackcurrant juice
a couple spoonfuls of concentrated beef stock
2 tsp dried thyme
10 crushed juniper berries
a small piece of dried, whole ginger (approx. 2 g)
5 black peppercorns
10 allspice berries
2–3 bottles of porter (not American hopped or smoked)
a couple of prunes

Ingredients for gravy, see p. 123

Directions

Brown the steak in butter and oil and place it in a
cast-iron pot. Add all the ingredients.

   Let simmer over low heat while covered for 45
minutes, and then flip the steak over.

   After another 45 minutes of simmering, measure
the inner temperature with a meat thermometer. At
160–170°F (70–75°C), the steak is ready, but ideally
you should let it rest for a moment in the juices.

   Mix the gravy with an immersion blender (but
remove the ginger first) and make a gravy from it—
see recipe on p. 123.

Serving

Serve the steak with gravy (that's where all the
flavor is), jelly, fried small onions, cooked greens,
and root vegetables.

   Remember to cut the steak into thin slices
across the fibers when it's served, otherwise it will
be very tough.

Chili stew

Last year, I was a judge in a chili competition. Lots of extremely ambitious amateur chefs (most of them with just as much beard and almost as much belly as myself) stepped forward and asked us to try their creations. What struck me then was that the recipe isn't the most important thing when it comes to chili. A recipe can sound fantastic and still not turn out well, and vice versa. The touch means more, and sadly, that's difficult to convey through a cookbook. You'll have to try your way forward—and don't forget that your tongue and nose are your most important tools!

— 4 LARGE PORTIONS —

at least 2¼ lbs (1 kg) prime rib
preferably a couple of marrow bones (which
   applies to almost all meat recipes)
3-4 large yellow onions
10 garlic cloves
4 Italian sweet peppers or
   in an emergency use regular red peppers
a couple of fresh chilies, for example ½ habanero
   and a couple of jalapenos
a couple of different varieties and flavors of dried chili,
   for example 2 mulato or chipotle, ½-1 cascabel
   and ½ of a small strong, red rascal of choice
2-3 Guinness or similar stout
approx. 1 tbsp salt
a little Kikkoman soy sauce
a little (homemade) meat stock
½-¾ cup (100-200 ml) Rauchbier
maybe a little honey
oil and butter

Directions

Cut the meat into large pieces (about 2 x 2 in) and brown sharply in butter and oil.

Chop the onion, coarsely chop the garlic, chop the peppers and fresh chilies. Brown it all up thoroughly—some pieces can be allowed to burn.

Break up the dried chili a bit.

Place all the ingredients in a large cast-iron pot and let it simmer, very slowly, for a couple hours, until there's hardly a piece left of anything, but everything becomes a thick paste. Remember to stir regularly, especially near the end, and dilute with more beer (I think you should try a little Rauchbier) or meat stock if it becomes too dry.

If it's too runny, then boil uncovered while stirring until you get a thick paste.

Add a little more salt, soy sauce, pressed garlic, ground chili, beef stock, Worcestershire sauce, or more beer to taste. If you want to balance the strength with a bit of sweetness, add a spoonful of honey.

Note

The chili must be cooked in a non-enameled cast iron pot for the sake of the flavor. By far the absolute best chili I make is in the family's shieling where we let it simmer from an old tripod suspended over an open flame. It will also be richer if it's allowed to stand for 24 hours in the pot and is then heated up before enjoying.

Welsh rarebit

This dish was once viewed as a real luxury meal in English pubs,
and most likely the only Welsh recipe that made it into Escoffier's famous cookbook.
Nowadays it's not so popular, as it's seen as greasy and sloppy
—but for me those are pluses!

———————— 4 PORTIONS ————————

10½ oz (300 g) sharp, aged cheddar
approx. 1¾ tbsp (25 g) butter
approx. ¾ oz (20 g) flour
1 cup (250 ml) ale
2 tsp English mustard powder
a pinch of black pepper
a little cayenne pepper, optional
2–3 tsp Worcestershire sauce
3 egg yolks
4 slices of bread

Directions

Grate the cheese. Melt the butter in a pot and make a roux with the flour; it should simmer over low heat for a couple minutes. Whisk in the ale and let it simmer into a fairly thick sauce.

Add the cheese and stir until it's melted. Season with spices and Worcestershire sauce.

Set in a water bath. Whisk in the egg yolks and increase the heat until it becomes a thick, slightly glossy, and hard-to-whisk batter (just above 140°F (60°C). Remove from heat quickly so that it doesn't separate.

Lightly toast four slices of bread. Place them in pans.

Pour the sauce on top and broil at the top of the oven so that it attains a lovely color; but the sauce shouldn't melt off too much (1–3 minutes).

Eat immediately with a strong, hoppy ale (or IPA)!

Note

If the batter cracks, it can only be saved with the hollandaise trick, see p. 155. If you can't save it, it's better to add in the egg whites as well and continue to heat and whisk until the batter becomes scrambled eggs— because that's also pretty good on toast.

Coq au vin

When it comes to cuisine quality, French cuisine comes first, and then nothing else even comes close to being number two or three. Then comes a plethora of other cuisines at spot number four: Indian, Italian, Turkish, German, Thai, Mexican, Spanish, Vietnamese, etc. Only during the past couple of years have I begun to view the Chinese culinary arts as equal to the French—although for the Chinese, it's not one set cuisine but a collection of several.

Here's the most French of all things: a rooster.

---

4 PORTIONS

---

1 rooster of about 7¾ lbs (3½ kg) (at least 6 months, and preferably of the cooking variety)

approx. 3½ tbsp (50 ml) wheat flour

6 oz (175 g) smoked bacon, sliced into thin strips

duck fat for frying

4–5 garlic cloves, chopped

red wine, enough to cover (Beaujolais or Bourgogne), 1–2 bottles

bouquet garni of 2 bay leaves, 4 sprigs of fresh parsley, 2–3 sprigs of fresh thyme

1 tsp rosemary, optional

1½ tsp black pepper

1–1½ tsp salt

24 small mushrooms (approx. 9 oz / 250 g), cleaned

20 pearl onions (tiny yellow onions) or small shallots, peeled

¼–½ cup (50–100 ml) beurre manié (wheat flour and butter stirred together), optional

2–3 tbsp eau de vie or brandy (or 1 tbsp Marc de Bourgogne)

Directions

Carve the rooster anatomically into legs, drumsticks, wings, and breast pieces. Slice the breasts in half lengthwise. (If you have a large pot, let the carcass cook with the meat. Otherwise, you can boil it separately and then reduce the stock and add it to the pot.)

Dust the meat with flour.

Fry the bacon in a little duck fat and then remove, but don't pour away the grease.

Brown the rooster in the bacon grease, together with the garlic.

Place the bacon and rooster in a large cast-iron pot and pour in the wine.

Add the herbs and salt. Bring to a boil and skim the foam then let simmer for about an hour (longer if the rooster is older and larger, less if it is younger and smaller).

Add the mushrooms and onions.

Let everything simmer until the meat is tender (30–45 minutes).

Remove the rooster, onions, and mushrooms and keep warm.

Strain the sauce and reduce it to just the right strength and flavor. (If it is too runny, thicken with beurre manié.) Bring to a boil. Season with liquor and with any additional herbs or spices, if needed.

Place the rooster and the vegetables in a clean pot and pour the sauce on top.

Serving

Should be served with a good rustic bread only. To serve it with potatoes, pasta, or rice would be an abomination!

Note

The recipe requires a proper rooster, with real muscle fibers, which will be tough before being simmered for at least half an hour or so. A one-year rooster is best, but a six-month one also works well, especially if it's a real, French breed such as Hubbard. Using chicken-like young roosters will make any recipe that calls for chicken tastier, but this doesn't work for coq au vin. The light, loose meat doesn't actually taste as good in red wine.

Tip 1

The legs are the most flavorful in coq au vin, so if you have two roosters, you may want to save the breast pieces for another dish and use the legs for this one.

Tip 2

You can also make a delicious burgundy stew based on the same recipe, if you swap the rooster for prime rib.

Mettbrötchen or Hackepeter

During Easter 1986, when I was fifteen years old, I spent a couple weeks in East Berlin. We were a group from the Catholic youth club which, led by my sister, went to visit a friend whose father was stationed at the American embassy there. At the same time we also befriended an East German youth club. We took turns preparing dinner on alternating evenings: we served them Swedish meatballs and they served us similar *Berliner Bouletten*. But there was one thing that they kept to themselves in a back room: a large bowl of "Mett," or "Hackepeter," as it is also called in Berlin. They weren't doing it to be stingy, but they were convinced our bellies wouldn't appreciate being stuffed with raw pork of DDR-quality. But mine did, and it was fantastically delicious.

Since then, I've found a number of good Mettbrötchen around Germany.

———— 6–12, DEPENDING ON HOW THICK YOU WANT THE MEAT ————

1⅓ lbs (600 g) ground pork with 35% fat
   content at most
¾–1 tsp salt
black pepper
1–2 yellow onions
3–6 rolls of the Brötchen kind

Directions

Ask your butcher to grind a couple of nice pieces of pork or grind it yourself (you get the best from ham steak).

Mix the meat with salt and freshly ground pepper. Slice the onions thinly.

Slice the rolls and cover both halves with a hearty layer of Mett—you don't need any butter (and I don't say that very often). Top with the onion slices and more freshly ground pepper and possibly a little extra salt.

Note

As a variation, you can grate part of the onion and mix it into the ground pork.

The FDA recommends not eating raw pork, since it can contain dangerous bacteria from modern butchering methods. Therefore, it's safest to use veal instead.

Southern German hare with Spätzle

From 1993 to 1994, I studied in Germany for the second time, this time in the town of Freiburg. Baden and the Black Forest have the best food in Germany with a lot of game. I soon fell in love with Baden hare and the wonderful side dish of Spätzle. The Germans also know to appreciate lingonberries as the finest of berries, which are served with deer, hare, and gamefowl.

4 LARGE PORTIONS

1 hare (3⅓–4½ lbs / 1½–2 kg)
1–2 bottles of red wine (preferably Baden Spätburgunder)
¼ cup (50 ml) red wine vinegar
1 bay leaf
6 lightly crushed juniper berries
2 cloves, whole
5 black peppercorns
1 tsp rosemary
½ tsp thyme, optional
1 scant tsp salt
2 carrots
2 parsley roots, optional
1 onion
5⅓ oz (150 g) bacon or smoked bacon
ground black pepper
butter
gravy, see recipe p. 123
+ possibly a little brandy and red wine

Spätzle

4 cups (14 oz / 400 g) flour
1 tsp salt
6 eggs
approx. 2 tbsp water
butter
fresh or preserved lingonberries
pear halves (from shop or home boiled)

Directions

Rinse the hare and cut it anatomically into a couple of large pieces. Pour in the wine, vinegar, spices, salt, and the chopped parsley root and onion. The marinade must cover the meat. Let stand in the refrigerator for 24–48 hours.

Fry the bacon in a large frying pan or pot and set aside.

Remove the hare from the marinade, but save the liquid. Wipe the meat dry and fry in the bacon fat until they attain a nice color. Grind plenty of black pepper on top. Return the bacon to the pan with the meat. Pour in the marinade and bring to a boil. Cover and let simmer. The hare is ready when the meat is tender and comes off the bone easily, about 1–1½ hours.

While the meat is simmering, stir together all the ingredients for the spätzle with a fork. Use enough water that the consistency becomes something between a dough and a batter. Let it rise for at least 15 minutes. Place a large pot with heavily salted water on the stove.

When the hare is done cooking, wrap it in foil to keep it warm and make a gravy from the liquid—such as the brown gravy recipe on p. 123, but it doesn't need as much flavoring near the end except for a little red wine and a splash of brandy.

Grate the spätzle dough with a "Spätzlebrett" (spätzleboard) over the boiling water. (If you don't have this tool, you can press the dough through a potato presser or place it on a cutting board and use a knife to shave down strips ¼ inch (5 mm) wide.)

When the spätzle floats to the top after a couple minutes, it's ready to be drained with a colander. Stir them around in a little butter so they don't stick together.

Serve the hare with the gravy, Spätzle, and lingonberries, preferably served in the cooked pear halves.

Note
I choose to serve the hare with the gravy on the side. If you want to make a traditional German Hasenpfeffer, the gravy should be made from *Sauerrahm* and half a cup of hare blood, which is poured over the hare and allowed to simmer for fifteen minutes.

How schnitzel turned baby Edward into a gourmet

When Edward was seven and a half months old, we vacationed in Austria.
While we were away, he was—according to the norm in 1971—moved from
jars of pureed baby food to the ones that contained small chunks. We introduced
him to this new food before we left, to avoid having to bring two different types of
baby food with us. He didn't like the bits in the food, but after a couple days, it was fine.
I fell ill upon arrival in Austria and then James promptly got the flu
and a high fever, so staying in a tent (which had been the plan) was out of the question.
We ended up staying in a lovely inn. As early as the first day,
Edward discovered that gruel wasn't the only blissful breakfast item.
Since we couldn't let him run loose in the dining room when he had finished his
gruel, we kept him sitting with us, and he soon discovered that we were eating.
Piercing howls alerted everyone in the dining room that
the poor child was probably starving to death, and so we gave him a small piece of
Brötchen to chew on. That disappeared quickly, and he loudly demanded more of the
same. Even his older sister's hardboiled egg soon found its way into the little baby's
mouth and was appreciated. When our health started improving, we started having
dinner at a nearby Gasthaus. We brought a jar of baby food with us for Edward,
which we asked the staff to heat. This was done quickly, far more quickly than
we got our food. So when our meal finally arrived, Edward's baby food was
long finished—and with screeching protests he made sure to get our food as well.
Pommes frites and Wienerschnitzel went down much more happily than the baby food,
and consequently, after a couple dinners with both
baby food and our food, he changed to adult food.
We brought a good number of unopened baby food jars home with us.

Ninnie Blom, Edward's mother

Edward Blom's Weincreme

After graduating in 1989, I studied for a year in Trier. It was an amazing time with wonderful friends, great experiences, and a lot of good food. The exchange rate at the time was one Deutsche Mark for 3.30 Swedish kronor, which made both food and Moselle's superior-quality wine incredibly cheap. And for the first time in my life, I had my own household and got to take care of the grocery shopping myself. Dr Oetker Weincreme became a dessert favorite. There wasn't just a bag with lemon fromage-like powder in the packaging but also a quarter bottle of white wine; you had to add cream yourself. (Later that year, I started bringing the dessert mixes home to Sweden and customs never realized there was wine in the packaging.) Today I've learned that traditional German Weincreme is more creamy and less fromage-y, but mine is more similar to the mix variety.

―――――――――――― 4 PORTIONS ――――――――――――

3 gelatin sheets
3 large egg yolks
½ cup (100 ml) sugar or corresponding amount
  of sugar substitute
1¼ cup (300 ml) intense, tart, and sweet German
  Riesling wine of good quality, preferably a
  Spätlese
1½ tbsp pressed lemon
approx. 1 tsp raw grappa (should strongly enhance
  the wine flavor but should itself
  remain unknown)
1¼ cup (300 ml) whipping cream, 40%
2 egg whites

Directions
Soak the gelatin leaves. Whisk the egg yolks with the sweetener in a large pot. Add the wine, lemon, and grappa.

Carefully heat while stirring vigorously until it thickens and the foam starts to settle (about 175°F / 80°C, but absolutely not above 183°F /84°C).

Melt the gelatin sheets into the pot while stirring and let cool.

Whip the cream until it forms stiff peaks. Whisk the egg whites into a stiff foam. Carefully fold into the cream, and fold the cream into the wine mixture.

Pour into a pretty bowl and cool in the fridge for at least 5 hours.

Decorate with lemonbalm leaves, red currants, or sliced apricots.

Rumtopf

Rote Grütze

When I was a child, I was fascinated by a small booklet attached to my parents' Stroh rum bottle that told of rumtopf. A couple years later we visited a friend, who was living as a monk in a Bavarian monastery, and in their garden the adults drank beer while I was given rumtopf with ice cream—which was probably stronger than the beer. It became a tradition for me to always mix rumtopf when on vacation in Germany. Rumtopf was originally a preservation method, which made it possible to enjoy fruits and berries all winter long. It is eaten with ice cream, cream, or semolina pudding. It is very alcoholic, so drivers should watch out.

Directions

Pour a strong rum and a little sugar in a large pot or glass jar at the start of summer.

Then, add in everything that matures in the garden from pre-summer to fall: cherries, raspberries, strawberries, apricots, currants, apples, plums, pears, etc. Core, rinse, peel, and divide into bite-sized pieces. Alternate with sugar and fill with rum so all the fruit and berries are covered.

After the last fill-up, the rumtopf should stand for at least 3 weeks. I recommend forgetting about the jar in the fridge until the end of November, when you should start enjoying the delicious fruits and berries.

That's when all the flavors of summer have blended and matured to perfection.

Rote Grütze is an incredibly simple dessert to throw together when guests pop by: a few berries from the freezer, a cup of wine, and a spoonful of potato flour. Since it's a German recipe, it naturally contains a couple splashes from the liquor cabinet.

1 lb (500 g) mixed sour berries (red- and blackcurrants, raspberries, blackberries, and cherries)—it's okay to use frozen berries, but let them thaw

1⅓ tbsp potato flour

¾ cup (200 ml) red wine (or even better ½ cup (100 ml) red wine and ½ cup (100 ml) cherry wine)

approx. 1 tbsp Kirschwasser, grappa, or fruit liquor —the amount is dependent on variety; it should only be a hinted taste

sugar substitute to taste or about ¼ cup (50 ml) sugar

at least 1¼ cups (300 ml) whipping cream 40% (doesn't work with 36% cheater's variety)

Directions

Mix the potato flour with the wine and liquor. Simmer while stirring so it becomes a thick cream. Pour the cream over a bowl of the berries and stir.

Add sweetener to taste until it's quite sweet and it balances the sourness.

Let cool in fridge. Serve with cream whipped in a mixer.

Note

A couple years ago, I made a genius discovery that if you whip the cream in a mixer instead of with a whisk, the result is far more compact and creamy—similar to clotted cream. For many dishes—this one among them—I absolutely prefer this kind of cream.

St. Martin's day is the 10th of November, and has been celebrated with roast and wine throughout the greater part of Europe. For a long time, goose was the norm at celebrations all across Sweden, and the classic goose dinner—the combination of black soup, roast goose, and apple cake—was actually invented in a Stockholm restaurant during the 1850s. Today, apart from fraternities and secret societies, it is mostly the Lucullus-inspired residents of Skåne who preserve this lovely tradition. They sometimes replace the apple cake with spettekaka–the sweet egg cake you can see on p. 149.

Black soup

10-20 PORTIONS

2 cups (500 ml) goose blood—or blood from another animal

"giblets" from a goose (intestines, neck, wings, feet, and head)

1 red onion

approx. 2 tsp salt

1 bay leaf

1 heaping tsp whole cloves

1 heaping tsp whole white peppercorns

1-2 tsp allspice

3 liter mild beef bouillon, homemade or from cubes

8 oz (225 g) prunes

5 tart apples

½-¾ cup (100-150 ml) sugar

½ cup (100 ml) wheat flour

1 tsp ground ginger

¼ cup (50 ml) distilled white vinegar (12%)

¾-1¼ cups (200-300 ml) fortified wine (port wine, Madeira, or sherry)

½-¾ cup (100-200 ml) red wine

2 tbsp brandy

a little herb seasoning (thyme or marjoram), optional

Worcestershire sauce

possibly soy sauce

goose liver sausage

Directions

Rinse the giblets. Cut apart the heart and the crop.

Place everything (except the liver) in a pot with onion, salt, and the whole spices. Cover with bouillon. Bring to a boil and skim off the foam. Simmer until the crop is tender (2–3 hours). Let the liver simmer as well during the last few minutes. Strain, but save both the liquid and the crop.

Meanwhile soak the prunes in about ¼ cup (50 ml) water for 1 hour.

Peel and core the apples and cut them into wedges.

Boil the sugar, apples, and prunes with the water the prunes soaked in, until everything is quite soft.

Strain the blood and whisk the flour into it. Add a little of the cooled liquid from the crop.

Boil about a liter of the liquid in a large pot. Stir in the blood mixture.

Carefully heat and let simmer for 10 minutes while stirring vigorously and constantly. If it becomes too thick, add more hot crop liquid.

Near the end, add ginger, the crop, and the fruit with its liquid (but save a few prunes and apples for serving).

Clear and chop the crop finely and add to the soup. Add white vinegar, wine, and cognac to taste.

It can be a little tricky to achieve the right flavor toward the end. A little more salt may be needed, sugar, stock, wine, brandy, or a little Worcestershire sauce, soy sauce, and herbs. The soup does gain a lot from being allowed to rest in the refrigerator and then heating.

Serve with goose liver sausage and the rest of the apple slices and prunes.

Enjoy with Madeira.

Note

In restaurants today, it's common to see the giblets served on the side, so each person can serve themselves. But in his day, Hagdahl suggested that the chef should be the one to clean the meat from the giblets instead and put it in the soup near the end of the preparation. This inevitably makes it easier for the guests and makes the soup much richer.

Roast goose

1 goose of 9–11 lbs (4–5 kg)
apples
prunes
salt and black pepper

Directions
Rub the goose with salt and pepper. Fill it with apples and prunes.
Roast in the oven at 325°F (160°C) for 3–4 hours, depending on size.
The internal temperature should be 185°F (85°C). Pour water over the goose regularly. (You should also
refill the roasting pan with water—if there's only fat left, the gravy will taste burnt.)
Served with red cabbage or Brussels sprouts, potatoes are a possibility, as well as gravy (see p. 123).

Note
The broth from the goose most likely consists of 80 percent fat. You'll have to separate this
and only use the broth at the bottom for the gravy.
Strain the fat and pour it into glass jars. Let it cool in the fridge to use in cooking. It's even better than
duck fat and is suitable for almost all types of cooking.

Gunilla and Edward's wedding snaps

For our wedding reception, I made my own snaps. It was supposed to have a fragrance of flowers and romance, and the majority of the spices are traditional aphrodisiacs. In addition, I customized the flavor to include my soon-to-be wife's favorite spices, with the intention that it would appeal to both women and men. It markedly differed from the recipes of the 1800s, which dominate today's brännvin offerings, but it probably would not have been considered original during the 1600s and 1700s. I made essences of all the spices (see description of Spiced brännvin snaps on p. 13) and supplemented them with rose water (which can be found in Oriental grocery stores). Then I combined them into just the right flavor. The goal was that no one spice would dominate but that the liquor would have a blended flavor in which all played an equal part. Roses, however, have such strong perfumes that they will dominate the fragrance. Of course, it's easier to create an essence from all the spices at once, but then you have less control over the finished product.

dried (or fresh) elderflower
fresh lemon balm
dried rosemary
a couple of splashes of rose water
a little violet root
a little Sweet gale
a little genuine vanilla
extremely small amount of Gentian root (not for bitterness,
    but just to give a hint of a bite to the aftertaste)

Use the essences to flavor a brännvin diluted to about 30% of alcohol.
    Add 2 tsp of clear blossom honey for every 3 cups (750 ml) of finished brännvin

The wedding dinner menu
The menu for our wedding dinner on June 17, 2011.
We came up with the ideas and a chef we know executed them perfectly.
Calligraphy and concept for the menu card: Barbara Bunke.

Love potions and love food

In most cultures, there's been a belief that certain foods, herbs, or drinks can act as aphrodisiacs—meaning to increase the man's sexual prowess, to boost the woman's libido, or to make the heart of the opposite party burn with desire.

Food and love have always belonged together: in the Bible "they ate together" can be a symbol for lovemaking. Food and procreation are our strongest drives, both of which spur the brain's pleasure center. The effects of food, love, and alcohol resemble and reinforce each other.

Food is considered an aphrodisiac for numerous reasons:
• The magic of similarities: if the food item resembles something indecent, such as asparagus, cucumber, artichoke, wild strawberry, sweet potato, caviar, eggs, and animal testicles—or rice, which of course is still tossed over the bridal couple.
• Precious foods—such as truffles, saffron, and exotic fruits—have always been considered to have magical, exciting qualities. A significant other spending money on a meal in itself creates

a special feeling of romance. And thanks to the placebo effect, anything that is expensive enough (such as reindeer antler powder) stimulates.
• Measurable effect: applies to chocolate, ginseng, maybe even asparagus, and alcohol, which releases one's inhibitions. Just remember that "wine is a false friend that increases desire, but inhibits ability"!
• Light dishes that feel romantic, without magical or pseudo-medical reasons: fish rather than beef, fruit over pudding, a light, white wine rather than a heavy, red one.

The most popular love food embraces all these points. Champagne is the lightest and most bubbly of all alcoholic beverages, and it's expensive to boot. You can have scores of oysters without it sitting heavily, and they contain substances to stimulate potency, feel like magic, and are, nowadays, quite pricey.

That they're difficult to open and may also contain a pearl makes them that much more exotic. So if you don't want to prepare a whole love menu, content yourself with oysters and champagne!

After-love drink

This recipe is taken from a book my sister
and brother-in-law received when they got married,
which they kindly lent to me prior to the "Love in a pot"
episode of a radio show.

*"Pour a quarter glass of Maraschino [cherry liqueur] into a
Madeira glass, one egg yolk, a quarter glass of cognac. Serve
without mixing—the egg yolk is not to be broken. Should be
swallowed in one go. Recommended warmly by my friend
Baron de M . . ."*

From *Venus in the kitchen— or Love's Cookbook* by Pilaff
Bey, 1953

Love buds
—truffle scented white asparagus with seared scallops and saffron hollandaise

Three for two, a love meal

I often receive requests on Twitter and Facebook from young gentlemen
who wish to cook a romantic dinner for the ladies of their hearts.
Here is a suggestion for a three-course meal for two.
The appetizer recipe was created by Ellen Wästfelt and myself for the episode "Love in the Pot"
when we were doing *Menu* for the Swedish radio in 2010. The episode was about
aphrodisiacs and romantic food and drink; we even brought a sexologist on the show as an expert.

--------------------- 2 PORTIONS ---------------------

Asparagus

1 bunch of white asparagus
½ tsp salt per quart (liter) of boiling water
1 pat of butter
1 small pinch of sugar
a couple of splashes of white wine, optional
truffle

Hollandaise sauce

10½ tbsp (150 g) butter
3 egg yolks
1–1½ tbsp white wine vinegar (or dry white
    wine for a less sour flavor)
½ tbsp pressed lemon, optional
¼ tsp white pepper
0.5 g crushed saffron
¼ tsp cayenne pepper, optional
approx. ½–1 tsp salt
½ cup (100 ml) whipping cream, optional
6 scallops
salt, olive oil

Directions

Peel the asparagus with an asparagus or
potato peeler. Start below the bud and
continue downward. The peel is not
chewable. So be careful.

The last half-inch at the bottom should be
cut off completely. (The peel and the ends
can be used to make a soup.)

Tie the asparagus into bunches with cooking
twine and boil them for 8–15 minutes (depending
on how thick they are) in water with salt, butter,
sugar, and possibly wine. (Ideally, you should use
an asparagus pot or asparagus steamer.)

Meanwhile, melt the butter for the sauce and set aside.

Mix the egg yolks, vinegar, lemon, and spices in
a pot. Heat the egg mixture in a water bath while
stirring vigorously until it thickens.

Add the melted butter extremely slowly while
continuing to whisk. Add salt to taste.

For a fluffier sauce: Make a Mousseline instead
by whisking ½ cup (100 ml) cream and folding it
into the hollandaise just before serving.

Rub the scallops with a little salt and olive oil.
Sear in hot frying pan or grill pan until they gain
a nice color.

Remove the asparagus, snip off the cooking twine,
and serve on a large plate. Sprinkle finely grated
truffle on top. Serve with the scallops and the sauce.

Note

Asparagus should be white, thick, freshly harvested, and carefully
cooked. It's an amazing delicacy around which entire celebrations are
centered in Germany. Some asparagus is a little too thin, and merchants
often let imported asparagus dry out because they don't know how to
handle it. Some cookbooks recommend cooking times that are much too
long. In other words: be choosey when buying and don't overcook. Green
asparagus is a vegetable; white asparagus is one of the most delicate
main courses that exists!

How to save a hollandaise
Emulsion sauces, such as hollandaise and béarnaise,
have a tendency to crack. Fortunately, all is not lost.
The secret is to pour in a little
warm water or wine while whisking quickly
until the sauce bonds again.

Snuggling by the pots and pans

Aphrodisiacs are all well and good, but a romantic dinner is more than just the food. The mood is also created by candles, ambient music, fine table settings, and fresh flowers.

The actual cooking can also be sensual. But creating perfect food with plenty of breaks for embraces and fiery kisses does require good multitasking skills! If the food goes to hell, the mood can also be ruined—so a good piece of advice is to avoid any overly-complicated dishes if you're going to cook them together.

Duck à la Edward Blom

My variation of the classic dish Duck à l'Orange, in which Pimm's (that most British of all summer drinks) features heavily. This is a recipe that I have developed and improved on over a period of fifteen years.

— 2 PORTIONS —

1 duck breast (approx. ¾–1 lb / 350–400 g)
2 organic oranges
black pepper, salt
a small shallot, finely chopped, optional
½–¾ cup (100–200 ml) Pimm's No 1
½ cup (100 ml) chicken stock (or broth)
2¾ tbsp (40 g) butter for frying
1 tbsp wheat flour
¾ cup (200 ml) whipping cream
1 tbsp Kikkoman soy sauce
a splash of concentrated chicken stock, optional

Directions

Remove the orange part of the peel from ¼ of the orange and finely chop. Chop the flesh of 2 oranges.

Score a diamond pattern across the fatty part of the duck breast with a sharp chef's knife. Brown the duck on both sides in a hot iron frying pan with a little butter. Add a little salt and coarse ground black pepper.

Let the orange peel fry for a couple of seconds (and if you like, fry a shallot as well). Then add the chopped oranges and half the Pimm's, which should cook for a couple minutes.

Place the duck breast in an oven proof pan, skin side down, and stick an oven thermometer in the middle. Place the pan in the oven at 200–210°F (90–100°C).

Boil the pan with the chicken stock (or broth) and save the gravy.

Flip the duck breast over after about 15 minutes. When the inner temperature is about 140°F (60°C), remove the duck breast from the oven, wrap in aluminum foil, and let rest.

Brown the butter. Add the flour and cook together. Pour in the cream (heated), a little at a time while whisking. Then add the soy sauce and the gravy from the frying pan, as well as the juices from the oven pan and half the orange flesh.

Boil the sauce while whisking and then strain. Reduce the sauce until it's almost as thick as béarnaise. Sample and add the rest of the Pimm's, salt, black pepper to taste, and possibly a little concentrated chicken stock.

Remove the duck breast from the foil. Fry the skin side quickly (about half a minute) in a frying pan over medium-high flame so that the skin becomes crispy.

Cut the breast into ¼ inch-thick slices across the fibers. Serve on warmed plates and decorate with the remaining chopped orange.

Gravy, sweet peas, a couple braised shallots, and even Hasselback potatoes or other baked potatoes are good on the side—as is a light and delicate Bourgogne.

Amorous chocolate mousse with a bite of chili

This chocolate mousse has a strong flavor but a very smooth consistency,
and a little bite of chili at the end—like love itself.
In my mind, it's the perfect end to a romantic dinner.

---

2 PORTIONS

5$\frac{1}{3}$ oz (150 g) dark chocolate, about 70% cocoa
2 egg yolks
½ cup (125 ml) strong coffee
barely 1 sherry glass of dark rum
¾-1¼ cups (200-300 ml) whipping cream, 40%
should become about 1$\frac{2}{3}$ cups (400 ml) when whipped
1-2 egg whites
a couple of drops of chili essence, which should preferably be made the day before (see below)
a couple of dashes essence of real vanilla

Directions

Melt the chocolate in a water bath. In a bowl, whisk the egg yolks and coffee. Heat the mixture in a water bath while stirring constantly, until it thickens (175°F/ 80°C), after which it should immediately be removed from the heat so it doesn't turn into scrambled eggs.

Whip the cream. Whisk an egg white— two if you'd prefer a fluffier mousse.

Stir the melted chocolate into the egg mixture. Add rum, chili essence, and vanilla to taste, but do so sparingly: the chili should only be hinted at and should in no way dominate. Let the chocolate cool, but it should not harden.

Fold first the whipped cream and then the whisked egg white into the chocolate; use large motions.

Pour into a beautiful crystal bowl and let stand in the refrigerator until the mousse has solidified (3–4 hours).

Serving

Serve with a dollop of newly whipped cream and raspberries, for example—or mango slices, fresh figs, or even passion fruit. And serve with a fortified wine that has a note of its cask and the flavor of rum raisin and dark berries.

Note

I personally use 90% chocolate, because I think it tastes better and to get a lower GI. This creates two problems:
1. some guests think that it becomes too bitter that way.
2. The mixture of chocolate and egg separates.

The latter problem can be solved by increasing the amount of egg yolk and coffee from the start. If it still separates, it can be saved by slowly adding hot water while stirring vigorously until the fat and liquid bond again into an emulsion. The batter must be completely smooth before the whipped cream and egg white can be folded in, otherwise the mousse will become grainy.

Chili essence

2 fresh, red chilies
approx. ¼ cup (50 ml) unflavored vodka

Remove the seeds and the stem from the chilies. Slice the chilies thinly and place in a glass jar. Pour in enough liquor to cover the chilies and cover with the lid. Let it stand for a couple days, but if needed, it can be ready after only an hour. Strain away the chilies and keep the essence, which will last for many years.

Lobster aspic

I don't understand why aspics and other jelly dishes have fallen out of favor,
Jelly is both delicious and healthy, but above all, aspics are so beautiful—like an aquarium,
where you can see the different ingredients swimming around. But, if one wishes to make the aspic
according to all the rules of the art and get the broth completely transparent, it will take time
—far more time than what the result is worth. So this is one of those dishes that works
best if one has a small kitchen staff waiting at home.

———— 8 APPETIZER PORTIONS, A BIT MORE AS A BUFFET DISH ————

3 lobsters (or 2 lobsters and a couple of pieces
   of lumpfish)
1½ quarts (1½ liters) fish or shellfish broth
½–1¼ cups (100–300 ml) sherry
spices to taste, for example a knife tip cayenne
   pepper, a splash of Tabasco, a couple of dill seeds,
   1 tsp chopped dill, some herbs, a splash of
   Worcestershire sauce, a little pressed lemon
20 gelatin sheets
3–5 tbsp brandy
9–15 egg whites
lemon
pepper, cayenne pepper, salt

Garnish
1–2 eggs
a little cucumber, dill, and other vegetables
6 oysters
shellfish
a little truffle, optional

Directions
Break the lobsters and save the meat. Save
all the shells you are cleaning out.

Boil the shells and discarded pieces from the
lobster in the liquid for at least 30 minutes. If
you have other discarded shellfish or pieces of
fish at home then add that to the pot, too.

Strain the liquid, add sherry, and season until it tastes glorious. This liquid makes up the
soul of the dish and so it has to be delicious.

Soak the gelatin sheets for at least 5
minutes. Melt the gelatin into the liquid and
stir it in properly.

Whisk 1 tbsp brandy with 3 of the egg whites. Whisk
the marinade into the liquid and simmer, but don't boil.

Let stand for 15 minutes and then strain again
through a fine cheesecloth. This is somewhat tedious,
but it's done to make the jelly as clear as possible.

Repeat the procedure with the egg whites,
simmering and straining until the liquid is completely
transparent—this requires three to five rounds.

Let the gelatin liquid, known as the jelly from
here onward, cool.

Cut the lobster tail into pieces and let it rest for a
moment in a mixture of lemon juice, a little pepper,
a little cayenne pepper, and a tiny amount
of salt.

Pour a little of the jelly into the bottom of an
aspic mold. Wiggle the mold around so the jelly
sticks to the sides. Garnish with the lobster pieces, dill, beautifully trimmed vegetables, halved
lemon slices, oysters, and truffle. Everything that is
beautiful and luxurious will do! Remember when
garnishing that the aspic will be tipped upside
down—so put the most good-looking items in the
bottom of the mold. Let it set in the fridge.

In batches, add in more "filling" (lobster, other
shellfish, fish, vegetables, egg slices, and more) and
jelly. Let it set in the fridge between batches.

Let stand in the refrigerator for at least 10 hours. Tip
out when ready to serve by pouring warm water on the
outside of the pan and then tinkering a little with a small,
sharp knife. Finally turn it upside down with a bang.

Serve as an appetizer, ideally garnished with dollops of piped mayonnaise from a pastry bag—and
paired with a really good white wine.

Fried smelt

Some dishes are perfect for dinner—as long as you don't have to cook them yourself!
In the olden days, smelt was fished from rowboats using large nets on Strömmen,
the bay in central Stockholm, and was something of the city's "signature dish."
But the small, slimy fish are infinitely difficult to clean—especially if you, like
Dr. Hagdahl, think the backbone should be removed.
They can also make your hands reek of cucumber for days—which is why the dish's popularity
declined so rapidly when people ceased to have servants who took care of the cooking.
It's sad, because they're really, really tasty—and cheap.

1 ⅓ lb (600 g) smelt
2 eggs
1 package of breadcrumbs
salt
pepper
plenty of butter

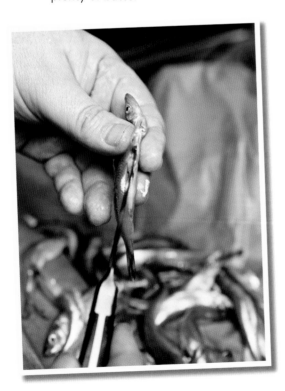

Directions

Clean the smelt from their packaging. (I usually keep the heads while frying, but the heads are not tasty to eat and should be cut off when eating.)

Dip the fish in a whisked egg and roll them quickly in breadcrumbs with salt and pepper. Fry quickly in plenty of butter.

When Gunilla and I ate smelt one weekday evening, we didn't have any pilsner at home and we didn't feel like drinking water. But what wine should be drunk with butter-fried small fish? We decided to see if we could verify the saying "champagne goes with everything." We were so pleased with the combination that now we could never consider drinking anything else with our smelt dinners.

Note
Smelt doesn't really require servants. Our favorite fish dealer, Pär-Anders Bergqvist, at Hav (Sea) in Stockholm's Hötorgshallen market tipped us off that if you choose small smelt, they can actually be cooked and eaten as they are, without cleaning—and it does actually work. So maybe smelt will experience a renaissance.

Blanc-manger à la Hagdahl

This dish has been beloved since the Middle Ages and is the predecessor of crème bavaroise and, consequently, to later inventions such as panna cotta, mousse, and more. "A very valued dish even on the finest of tables," wrote Charles Emil Hagdahl (see p. 24) himself. Here we present Hagdahl's original recipe, with the only difference being that I use gelatin sheets instead of preparing a "jelly substance" out of veal. Since this old variation doesn't contain cream, it's perfect to cook in places where you don't have a refrigerator. The flavor is utterly fantastic (I think), but even this dish is extremely demanding. The liquid has to be pressed through a cheesecloth, and that's a heavy and messy job.

---

4 oz. (110 g) sweet almonds
6 bitter almonds
5 oz. (150 g) sugar
1 lemon
1 large pinch of coriander (seeds)
clarified substance from calf feet (3-4 gelatin leaves)

Directions

The almonds are to be blanched, peeled, and mashed into a dough, while being given a little water so the mixture doesn't become oily. The sugar and 17 thumbs (about 1¾ cup / 420 ml) water should be place over the fire in a pot along with the (whole) peel and half (the juice from) the lemon and the coriander; all of it should stand and rest for ½ an hour (over low heat). Then remove the lemon and coriander and pour the rest over the almonds. Strain several times through serviette (sic!). As much substance (gelatin) is added as is required, which is known through experimenting. Pour either into small cups or in a large mold and then allow to harden on ice.

This blanc-manger, which is the oldest original, is without doubt one of the best.

From Charles Emil Hagdahl's
Kok-konsten som vetenskap och konst, 1879

Note
A simpler and just as delicious result can be achieved by running the almonds in a mixer for 10 minutes together with the strained preserve and about 3½ tbsp (50 ml) boiling water.

You have to wring the liquid out of the cheesecloth the first time. A regular cotton towel will hold better than a cheesecloth, and you really don't need to sacrifice a nice serviette. The subsequent attempts to strain the almond milk are probably done just to get a clearer pudding.

The Vibrant 1800s

I love the 1800s! Everything from Gluntarne's crazy student pranks during the 1840s to the grand banquets at luxury hotels in the overloaded new fashions of the fin de siècle, with gold, elaborately wrought plasterwork, crystal chandeliers, palm trees, and burgundy wallpaper. During the 1800s, the freedom to trade in Sweden increased, which gave us a never-before-seen economic boom. People wore tailcoats, smoked cigars, quenched their thirst with arrack punch, listened to Bellman choirs, put colorful ribbons—worn as insignia of honor and rank—on each other, and ate at gigantic *smörgåsbords*.

Even common people, who had previously gotten 90 percent of their nutritional intake from grains, experienced improvements. For the bourgeoisie, even the junior civil servants, it was completely possible to have every meal in a restaurant. Champagne and French wines cost a pittance, people wallowed in oysters, caviar, and wild fowl. Never has the art of Swedish cooking been on such a level. Everything was organic and handmade. Every sauce was made from stock, which had been cooked for days from pounds of bones and trimmings, and people were allowed to partake of dishes that were so advanced that up to ten servants could have been working on them in the kitchen.

Bern's salonger in Stockholm epitomizes the lifestyle I associate with the 1800s —and it was in the classic Red Room, immortalized through August Strindberg's novel of the same name, that we took the photographs of my favorite dishes from the era.

Toast Pelle Janzon

"So simple and so wickedly tasty!" is how a good friend described this dish. And so Edwardesque, I could add, and yet it was only fairly recently that I was enlightened about its existence. The toast was named after the opera singer Per "Pelle" Janzon, who was a singer at the Stockholm Opera at the end of the nineteenth century. He was enamored with food and was known to host sumptuous "sexor" (after parties with late-night suppers) that could last until morning.

— 4 PORTIONS —

10-14 oz (300-400 g) beef tenderloin
1 red onion
chives
4 slices of toast
butter
4 large egg yolks
3 oz (80 g) whitefish roe
white pepper and salt

Directions

Trim the beef tenderloin and cut it into four thick slices across the fibers.

Place each slice between two sheets of plastic wrap. Roll and pound the meat with a rolling pin, so each slice becomes very thin.

Chop the onion and the chives finely.

Cut the crusts from the bread and fry the slices in plenty of butter.

Assemble each Toast Pelle Janzon by placing the bread slice on a plate and topping with first the meat, then red onion, an egg yolk, and a dab of whitefish roe.

Sprinkle with chives, freshly ground white pepper, and salt.

Serving

Serve with porter or a heavily hoppy and malted pilsner and snaps (Linie or OP, for example).

Sole Walewska

This dish is one of the quintessential old-fashioned, French food luxuries, named after either Napoleon's mistress or his daughter-in-law. Like so many classics from the grande cuisine of the 1800s, this dish is now almost completely forgotten in its homeland but has survived in Sweden where it has found its own style. There are many different elements to the dish and it costs a pretty penny, but it's definitely worth it.

--- **4 PORTIONS** ---

2 lobsters
1½ lbs (650 g) fillet of sole
1–1½ tbsp butter
¾ cup (200 ml) white wine
approx. 2 tbsp (30 ml) fish bouillon
¾–3 ½ oz (20–100 g) truffle
1¾–2 oz (50–60 g) grated gruyere

Lobster sauce

lobster shell
oil for frying
1 piece of celeriac (approx. 3½ oz / 100 g)
1 medium carrot (approx. 3½ oz / 100 g)
1–1½ yellow onions
2 tbsp tomato paste
approx. 1¼ cup (300 ml) of the fish broth
just about 1–1¼ cup (250–300 ml) whipping cream
approx. ⅓ cup (70 ml) brandy
salt
cayenne pepper

White wine sauce

1–2 shallots
approx. 3 tbsp butter
2 heaping tbsp wheat flour
½ cup (100 ml) white wine
approx. ¾ cup (200 ml) of the fish broth
¾ cup (200 ml) whipping cream
salt and pepper
possibly a couple of splashes of vermouth or
   dry sherry

Mashed potatoes

2¼ lbs (1 kg) potatoes
at least 2 oz (50 g) butter
4 egg yolks
salt, pepper, grated nutmeg
a little of the potato water

Directions

Read through the entire recipe first. The different parts of the dish (sauces, mashed potatoes, etc) have been written out one by one to avoid chaos. But you gain time by alternating between the various elements.

Remember to taste and to try to achieve perfection in every part: it must be a very good wine sauce, a wonderfully delicious lobster sauce, and heavenly mashed potatoes for the end result to fulfill its promise.

Break open the lobster and remove all the meat from tail and claws. Cut the tails in half lengthwise. Chill the tails and the claw meat.

Save each of the following in separate containers: 1) all of the shells from the back and the large claws, 2) all the other edible leftovers (lobster butter, roe, meat from the legs, etc., 3) the inedible "scraps" (small claws, chest, etc).

Roll up the sole fillets and place them in a greased pot. Add a pat of butter, fill with wine and fish bouillon until covered. Bring to a boil and simmer while covered 6–7 minutes.

Remove from the broth and place someplace cold, but keep the fish broth for later.

(The recipe continues on the next page.)

Sole Walewska

Lobster sauce

Rinse the lobster shells, place them on a baking sheet, and dry in the oven at around 200°F (100°C) 40–60 minutes. In a large mortar, crush the pieces into small flakes.

Cover the bottom of a spacious pot with oil and heat up. Add the crushed shells and fry for 7 minutes while stirring. Add diced celeriac and carrot and finely chopped onion. Fry 4–5 minutes while stirring.

Take the pot off the heat. Add a dollop of tomato paste. Dilute with the fish broth.

Add the inedible scraps from the lobster (and any you have from the sole) and let it cook along for the flavoring.

Simmer 30–40 minutes while covered.

Strain. Pour in the whipping cream and brandy and reduce until it is a very thick sauce—stir to make sure it doesn't burn or stick.

Add in the remaining edible lobster you saved earlier—not the pretty tails and the claw meat—and blend with an immersion blender until smooth.

Add salt and a bit of cayenne pepper to taste.

White wine sauce

Chop the shallots finely and saute in butter until soft. Sprinkle with flour and cook for a couple seconds more.

Pour in the white wine and stir until the flour dissolves.

Add the fish broth and dilute with the fish broth and cream.

Simmer for at least another fifteen minutes. Then, strain away the onion. If it isn't a thick enough sauce, reduce. Add salt, pepper, and a little sherry or vermouth to taste.

Mashed potatoes

Peel and boil the potatoes. Drain, but save the water. Mash the potatoes.

Stir in the butter and egg yolks as well as the spices.

If the mashed potatoes are too thick to be able to pipe through a pastry bag, dilute with the potato water.

Assembly

Using a pastry bag, pipe the mashed potatoes along the rim of an ovenproof dish and brown in the oven (575°F / 300°C) for about 3 minutes.

Remove the dish from the oven and pour in a layer of the white wine sauce—enough to cover the bottom.

Place in the rolled sole fillets.

Add the halved lobster tails, lobster claws, and beautifully cut truffle slices.

Drizzle with the lobster sauce and cover with a layer of gruyere, but avoid covering the lobster tails—which should be left visible.

Bake at 575°F (300°C) until everything is nicely browned (about 3–7 minutes).

Note

Sole Walewska embodies the opulence, crystal chandeliers, champagne—yes, all the Baroque luxury that characterized Paris's best restaurants during the years the dish was created—an excess we can hardly imagine today. Of course, you can exchange the sole for saithe, fresh lobster for frozen, or even for shrimp, and the truffle for sautéed mushrooms—but as a good friend said: "If you want fish gratin, you can just buy it in the frozen section."

But even the great Escoffier says that you can substitute the lobster for crayfish, and he uses neither wine nor lobster sauce, but plenty of cheese sauce.

Punsch pudding

During the late 1800s, arrack punch (in Swedish) monopolized the bourgeois drinking habits in Sweden. There were students and officers who drank up to half a gallon a day! People drank it on so-called "punsch verandahs," made picnics with little punsch steamers, held patriotic punsch speeches, and eventually gained large punsch bellies. It was even poured into puddings—which is incredibly delicious!

———— 4–5 PORTIONS ————

5 gelatin sheets
1¼ cup (300 ml) Swedish arrack punsch
1 heaping tsp potato flour
1¼ cup (300 ml) room temperature whipping
    cream, 40%
4 eggs, divided
a couple of splashes of sugar substitute
    or 2 tbsp sugar

Directions

Soak the gelatin sheets. Combine half of the punsch with the potato flour and let simmer in a pot over low heat until it thickens.

Remove the gelatin sheets and melt them into the warm punch mixture. Pour in the rest of the punsch.

Whip the cream until stiff peaks form. Whisk the egg yolks with the sweetener and carefully stir into the cream.

Whisk the egg whites.

While they are being whisked, carefully fold the gelatin mixture into the egg-cream mixture. (To lessen the risk of creating "gummies" in the pudding, first take ½ cup (100 ml) of the egg-cream mixture and stir together with the gelatin mixture until it is completely absorbed.)

Finally, carefully fold the whisked egg whites into the mixture. Be careful not to let the air escape.

Refrigerate the pudding until it solidifies completely (at least four hours).

Note
If you want to create a real nineteenth-century atmosphere, then continue the evening with fine varieties of Swedish arrack punsch. But punsch shouldn't be drunk with the pudding, as the flavors will cancel each other out. Port wine or similar work best.

Anna von Krusenstierna,
Edward Blom and Gunilla Kinn Blom

Hummus with hazelnuts

Hummus is a delicious accompaniment to most things, and this is my interpretation
of the classic dip. If you want to make a complete meze meal, you can serve
the hummus with fresh-baked bread, olives, eggplant fried in olive oil
and garlic, plus herb cream cheese.

14–16 oz (400–450 g) boiled chickpeas
3 tbsp tahini
2 garlic cloves
½–1 tbsp pressed lemon
½ tsp sesame oil
¼–⅔ cup (50–75 ml) olive oil
¼ tsp paprika
½ tsp cumin
a few dashes of Tabasco
½ tsp salt (at least)
½ cup (100 ml) water, or preferably chickpea liquid
½ cup (100 ml) hazelnuts

Directions

If you've soaked and boiled the chickpeas, save
the boiled water. If you're using canned chickpeas,
throw away the liquid.

Mix the chickpeas, tahini, a pressed garlic clove,
lemon juice, oils, spices, salt, and half the water in
a mixer until it becomes a smooth paste.

Roast the hazelnuts in a dry cast iron pan for a
couple minutes, shaking the pan all the while. Add
a little oil toward the end so the shells darken but
don't blacken. Toss in a finely sliced garlic clove to
cook along.

Add the hazelnuts and garlic slices to the hummus. Run the mixer again so the hazelnuts are
chopped roughly.

Boil the rest of the water/liquid in the frying
pan and pour into the hummus. Stir.

If you want a runnier hummus, add more water
or oil. Add salt and maybe some spices to taste.

Cream cheese with peanuts

Making cream cheese by running cottage cheese in a mixer is something I learned at a party, when cheaper cream cheese could not be found. Crossing cream cheese with peanuts is my own invention.

1 tub (500 g) of cottage cheese
½ tsp salt
1 pressed garlic clove
½–¾ cup (100–200 ml) peanuts (roasted and salted)
cream, optional

Directions

Run all the ingredients in a mixer until you get a perfectly smooth cream.

Add some of the peanuts toward the end if you want it to be more "chunky."

Dilute with a little cream or other liquid for a less solid consistency.

Let it stand in the fridge for a couple hours so the flavors have time to develop.

Blue and white sauce

I recently created this sauce when making ribs.
The ribs had a hint of American BBQ flavors, and this cool sauce was a fantastic complement.
Additionally, this recipe is a good way to make use of leftover cheese.

¼ cup (50 ml) mayonnaise
¼ cup (50 ml) (approx. 50 g) gorgonzola (the edges can be included)
¼ cup (50 ml) (approx. 50 g) chèvre (the edges can be included)
¾ cup (200 ml) sour cream
5–10 walnuts, chopped
1 tsp salt
black pepper, optional

Directions

Run the mayonnaise, cheese, and sour cream in a mixer. Stir in the nuts and add salt and pepper to taste.

Edward's five ice creams

When I started following the Montignac Method fifteen years ago, it basically caused me to cease using sugar, and the number of desserts available to me decreased. Now I had chosen the diet because I can easily choose to avoid sweets, but ice cream is an exception. That's when I started to make my own sugar-free ice cream, which has given rise to many varieties—some of which are presented here.

Base recipe, ice cream batter

If gelatin sheets are included, soak them for 5 minutes.

Whisk together the egg yolks and the whipping cream. Let simmer in a water bath (158°F [70°C] but not above 165°F [74°C]) while stirring constantly, until it becomes a semi thick batter and the foam begins to subside.

Remove from heat and stir in the gelatin sheets until they've melted.

Note

If you make the ice cream with a sugar substitute rather than real sugar, you'll have to add liquor so the batter doesn't stick to the ice cream maker. However, adding liquor to ice cream *with* sugar is also favorable, as it improves the taste.

Remember, the ice cream will not be as sweet as the batter, as the cold dulls the perception of sweetness.

My pink Montignac ice cream

Thanks to the rum, this ice cream is more like soft-serve. It doesn't lend itself well to freezing and should be eaten at once. Austrian rum is spiced and differs quite a lot from regular rum, and it's the one that fits this purpose.

2 gelatin sheets, optional
4 egg yolks
2 cups (500 ml) whipping cream
5 dried figs
½ cup (100 ml) juice from canned peaches
⅔ lb (225 g) strawberries
⅓ cup (66 ml) Austrian rum
   (such as Stroh or Balle) 50-60%
a dash of real vanilla extract
1 tbsp Swedish punsch
enough sugar substitute (or possibly sugar)
   to make it sweet

Directions

Make the ice cream batter following the base recipe.

Boil the figs in the peach juice until they are soft (about 10 minutes). Run the figs and the strawberries in a blender.

Add rum, vanilla, punch, and a little sweetener or sugar.

Stir all the ingredients together. Let cool (preferably to about 50°F / 10°C) and run in an ice cream maker until it gets the consistency of soft-serve ice cream.

Can be served with canned peaches, since you've already opened them anyway!

Rhubarb and punsch ice cream

A fresh rhubarb dessert with very little sweetness.

2-3 gelatin leaves for softer consistency, optional
3 egg yolks
1¼cup (300 ml) whipping cream
½ lb (250 g) rhubarb
⅓ cup (70 ml) Swedish punsch
1 tsp ground cinnamon
sweetener or ⅓–½ cup (75-100 ml) sugar

Directions

Prepare the ice cream batter following the base recipe.
   Cook the rhubarb into a compote (5–10 minutes).
   Whisk together the ice cream batter, rhubarb, punsch, cinnamon, and sweetener.
   Let cool (preferably to about 50°F (10°C) and run in an ice cream maker.

Licorice and absinthe ice cream with blood orange and star anise syrup

—— 4 PORTIONS ——

This is an elegant and somewhat unconventional dessert Gunilla and I composed when we had guests over last year. It was very fun to pick out licorice candies for the decorations . . .

3 gelatin sheets
1¼ cup (400 ml) whipping cream
4 egg yolks
¼ cup (50 ml) absinthe, 60% (if it is stronger, decrease the amount)
1 tbsp genuine licorice powder
1 tbsp honey
sugar substitute to taste (or 1½–3½ tbsp / 25-50 ml sugar)

Directions

Make the ice cream batter according to the base recipe.
   Stir in the absinthe, licorice powder, and honey. Add sweetener to taste.
   Let cool (preferably to 50°F/10°C) and run in an ice cream maker.

Blood Orange accompaniment

3 blood oranges
½–¾ cup (100-200 ml) water
10 star anise
2-3 tbsp absinthe
2 tbsp honey

Directions

Squeeze the blood oranges. Simmer the juice, water, star anise, and the absinthe for 15–30 minutes while covered.
   Strain (but you can keep a couple of the star anise for decoration).
   Add the honey. Boil uncovered while keeping an eye on it until the syrup is viscous (about 15 minutes).

Serving

Cut the flesh from 2 oranges into raspberry-sized pieces. (Fillet them first if you have the energy.) Distribute on plates.
   Pour the syrup over the oranges and drizzle decoratively on the plate.
   Add a couple of scoops of ice cream.
   Decorate with licorice and star anise.

Roquefort ice cream

This ice cream is wonderfully delicious and creamy, but it's not sweet—so it should be viewed as an alternative to the cheese tray rather than as a dessert.

1¼ cups (300 ml) whipping cream
4 egg yolks
7–9 oz (200–250 g) Roquefort or other bleu cheese
¼–½ cup (50–100 ml) roughly chopped walnuts
1 tbsp Madeira
1⅓ fl oz (40 ml) vodka

Directions
Make the ice cream batter in accordance with the base recipe.

When the batter has cooled somewhat, add in the cheese and mix until smooth.

Stir in the walnuts, Madeira, and liquor. Let cool (preferably to 50°F / 10°C) and then run in the ice cream maker.

Serve with a marmalade (for example, fig or pear).

Meat ice cream

—— 8 SMALL PORTIONS ——

About ten, fifteen years ago, we were talking about food trends over dinner. I was convinced that, in the future, there would be savory ice cream. "Ice cream is delicious, but why can't we have a few hearty flavors, instead of silly little trifles such as sweet berries?" We started brainstorming and I fell in love with the idea of meat ice cream—I was all fired up to register the company Meat Ice Cream Ltd. But the others were less in love with the project once they had sobered up the next morning . . . I hope you'll be more enthusiastic about this frozen steak tartare. You can eat it as an appetizer or palate cleanser.

1¼ cup (300 ml) whipping cream
4 egg yolks
⅓ lb (175 g) lean topside/minute steak
⅓ cup (70 ml) brandy
½ tbsp meat stock, optional
1 tsp Worcestershire sauce
½–1 tsp capers
1½ tbsp pickled beets
⅓ yellow onion or 1 shallot
1 tsp soy sauce
½ crushed garlic clove
¼ tsp black pepper
1 tsp salt

Directions
Make the ice cream batter in accordance with the base recipe.

Chop (or preferably grind) the meat and stir it into a little of the ice cream batter. Run in a mixer until it is very smooth—there can't be any pieces or membranes left.

Stir it into the rest of the ice cream batter and add the brandy, Worcestershire sauce, capers, ½ tbsp of the beets, onion, soy sauce, garlic, pepper, optional meat stock, and salt, and blend it again until smooth.

Add 1 tbsp finely chopped beet at the end and run in the ice cream maker.

A glass of red wine goes perfectly with this ice cream, but dark, strong beer at room temperature also works well.

Punsch Royal   Esoteric Solipsist   Bacon Old Fashioned

Berlin Morning   Hotel Oloffson's Rum Punch   Honey Bunny Blom

Esoteric solipsist

My good friend Martin Melin and I created this cocktail when absinthe was still forbidden throughout most of Europe. Our goal wasn't to mimic the flavor of absinthe, but its effect. Initially, it only consisted of the first three ingredients, but when a bartender at Richie sneered at our order and sarcastically remarked, "I might as well throw in some grappa too," we naturally gave it a shot—especially as grappa was the favorite drink of the third member of our gentlemen's club in those days: "Esoteric Solipsists."

¼ tequila
¼ Pernod
¼ Fernet Branca
¼ grappa

Directions
Mix all ingredients (without ice) with a spoon in a glass. Serve in a shaker. Knock it back or just sip.

Note
A *solipsist* is an individual who is convinced that he or she is the only thing that exists in the whole world, and that every other person and even the entire environment are all figments of one's own mind A state that can arise after too many esoteric solipsists . . .

Honey Bunny Blom

At the premiere of my TV show *Mellan skål och vägg,* our producer Peter Andersson arranged a party at his local pub. My stomach was destroyed after a magnificent brandy tasting we had attended while recording in Vadstena, and I could hardly drink any alcohol without getting pains in my abdomen. The only things that went down easily were egg and cream drinks.

Since I'd grown tired of the ones I knew by name, I asked the bartender for advice, and she promptly mixed a Caramel (created in 1998 by Ros-Marie Bille). I drank these for the rest of the evening. Sofie Larsson, the bartender, and I became friends and, at one New Year's, instead of bringing flowers, she brought a basket with a shaker, drinking glasses, and all the ingredients for Caramels.

A few years later, she composed this slightly sweeter variation of the Magic Bar and christened it Honey Bunny Blom.

²/₃ oz (20 ml) Frangelico
²/₃ oz (20 ml) Bailey's
²/₃ oz (20 ml) white cocoa liqueur
²/₃ oz (20 ml) whipping cream
a little honey
chocolate sauce for decoration

Direction
All the ingredients are first shaken with ice.

Pour into a frosted glass that has been decorated with chocolate sauce stripes.

If you want to, top the drink with a chocolate sauce heart.

Kristina Lindström, Lars Lundqvist, Elisabet Melin, Gunilla Kinn Blom, Edward Blom, Martin Melin

Edward at Hotel Oloffson

In the fall of 2010, I embarked on my seventh assignment to Haiti. Edward and
I were newly engaged and, despite an earthquake, a cholera epidemic, and political unrest,
he followed me to the capital city of Port-au-Prince. It was as good a proof of love as
anything, since Edward isn't the type to willingly put himself at risk—and Haiti isn't
exactly a tranquil vacation destination. But despite his constant fear of danger, he soon made
himself at home, and at that time he was probably Haiti's only tourist
(dressed in Panama hat and linen shirt, of course).
Between visits to tent camps, townships, and catholic services, we gathered at the legendary verandah at
the Hotel Oloffson [sic!], with other journalists, relief workers, missionaries,
businessmen, and all sorts of odd characters.
This is my "home away from home" when I'm in Haiti, and now also Edward's.
The Hotel Oloffson has a legendary drink on its cocktail menu: rum punch.
Edward often recreates it at home to remember our time together in the Caribbean.

Gunilla Kinn Blom

Hotel Oloffson's Rum Punch

At the Hotel Oloffson, the base for this drink is mixed beforehand. When you order, they just add the rum and shake with ice. If you try to find out what the recipe is, the bartender will suddenly become evasive. Rum, absolutely, lime, something to make it bitter, and something to make it red—but we couldn't get anything more than that out of him. American magazines have published recipes that don't seem very reliable. But in Arne Häggquist's 1982 classic *Största Cocktailboken*, we found the following recipe, which most likely is the original.

2 fl oz (60 ml) Barbancourt rum, 8-year-old
2 fl oz (60 ml) juice from a pressed lime
1 2/3 fl oz (30 ml) Grenadine
2–3 splashes of Angostura Bitters
½ spoonful of sugar

All the ingredients are shaken together and served in a tall glass with an orange wedge and ice. But if it's going to be as big as the one served at the Hotel Oloffson, you'll probably have to double the recipe.

Punsch Royal

This is the Blom household's signature drink. My wife and I drank it on our first date and as the bridal toast at our wedding reception—and I've managed to include it in several of the TV shows I've been a part of. Punsch Royal existed as early as the 1700s, but in those days a hot, freshly brewed arrack punch was topped off with a bottle of champagne.

Pour 1⅓–2 fl oz (40–60 ml) Swedish punsch (for example Kronan or Carlshamns flaggpunsch) into a large champagne flute.
  Carefully fill it up with cold champagne.

Berlin Morning
(BERLINER MORGEN)

This drink originated twelve years ago. A gang of German students and I had met in Berlin and partied through the night. By early morning, we were sitting in a swing—which was part of an outdoor dining area somewhere in Mitte. Five of my friends were already asleep, one was awake, I was just dozing off. But it was my round. My solution was to go to the bar and spontaneously order the following creation.

Pour 2 fl oz (60 ml) absinthe in a large glass. Fill up with Red Bull.
  Avoid ice, if it's going to be poured down the throats of sleeping people.

Bacon Old Fashioned

I first drank this bacon-flavored brunch cocktail at Bette Midler's New Leaf Bar in Uptown Manhattan. I then blended it in the TV show *Breaking News with Filip & Fredrik*. Unfortunately, liquor is seldom seasoned with meat: *myrbrännvin* (ant-infused aquavit), *bäverhojt* (beaver booze or castoreum liquor), and *märgtequila* (marrow tequila) are the only other varieties I know of.

1 sugar cube or 1 tsp maple syrup
2 fl oz (60 ml) bacon whiskey
a little soda water
2 splashes of Angostura Bitters
one twist of orange peel
a piece of crispy bacon for decoration

Directions
Combine the sugar cube or syrup, Angostura Bitters, and a little soda water in a glass. Stir. Fill the glass with ice.

Pour the bacon whiskey on top.

Add the orange peel and garnish with a strip of bacon.

How to make bacon whiskey
Fry strips of bacon until crispy and brown. Strain the fat. Let cool and pour the bacon into a bottle of bourbon whiskey.

Let stand at room temperature for about a week. Shake every now and then.

Place the bottle in the freezer for 24 hours and then pour the liquor through a sieve so that the fat is separated. By then, it should have given the liquor a bacon flavor.

Edwards midnight snack

This is the mother of all drunk munchies, and it's perfect for preventing hangovers after a long night of partying. It should be eaten when you get home from your escapades, with a large glass of milk, and only once you've reached the stage where you've completely lost your appetite for regular drunk eats, beer, brandy, nightcaps, or anything alcoholic at all.

Directions

Spread a thick layer of butter on a slice of bread. Add five Swedish anchovy fillets.

Throw on a crazy amount of mayonnaise, and top with plenty of slices of a good cheese.

Hangover lunch

There are many books with intriguing recipes that are said to cure hangovers.

To be honest, the only things that really help are: inducing vomiting, a suppository of Acetaminophen, resuming your alcohol drinking, or small pink pills called Optalidon, which are sold without a prescription at Spanish pharmacies.

But, even if food doesn't cure the hangover, it can at least make you feel a bit better, and that's where the recipe below fits in—although almost everything in this cookbook probably makes perfect day-after food. This dish isn't just good for hangovers—I've also used it successfully to self-medicate against sadness, love troubles, insomnia, and moderate anxiety. (My brother-in-law does, however, claim that you can get ileus from too much melted cheese—which of course guarantees that you forget all your other troubles.)

——— I PORTION ———

1 lb (500 g) hard cheese (all varieties work)
if you like, a little seasoning in the form of a splash of liquor, or a little nutmeg, caraway, chili, garlic, or similar.

Directions

Melt the cheese in the microwave on medium heat. Stir a couple of times so the outer parts don't harden.

Take it out while there's still an unmelted center.

Splash a little liquor or sprinkle some spices on top. Mash the unmelted center and stir everything around.

Eat with a spoon before the cheese hardens.

The ones who made this book and the ones who made it possible

Eva Hildén Smith took all the photographs and, from her own or our collective ideas, compiled them—and thus made this book into what it is. She has been tireless with her ideas, obtaining all sorts of fun props (everything from the lamb rib cage in the note at the beginning to her own husband dressed in Lederhosen), and giving great advice. She's been so positive all throughout, even though, time and again, she found our apartment in chaos, the cooking not even started, and several key ingredients still not purchased when she arrived each morning to begin taking photographs—once I was even asleep.

My wife, Gunilla Kinn Blom, helped out in developing some of the recipes, took part in all of the cooking, did most of the dish-washing, and went on many difficult shopping trips—it's not always easy to get hold of a French rooster, a sugarloaf, and a can of ghee on a Monday morning in Stockholm . . . She found all the locations, assisted at the photography sessions, reworked and improved the texts to the last moment and, not the least, worked hard with the translation and adaption into English. She has been an amazing source of ideas and a sounding board, and not least, my muse who has made the entire project possible.

Most of the photographs have been taken in Gunilla's and my home and mostly with our own things.

Pär Wickholm was responsible for the beautiful design and was so enthusiastic that he even took part in several of our photography sojourns. Jesper Lindberg, as an experienced editor, brought our original Swedish text to completion. Last but not least: a huge thanks to our Swedish publisher Johanna Kullman who took great initiative and gave me free reign to create this book.

Thank you . . .

—to everyone who has tried the recipes and thereby improved them considerably: The Blom, Dunér, Örndahl-Huss, Peeker, Mann, Melin, Nyman, Giritzlehner, Priebe, Döös, Birgander, and Nyberg-Jakobsson families and especially Hans Andersson, Fredrik Innings, and Per Lindström and family.
—to the friends who modeled!
—to all the people and venues who kindly lended us props.
—to Elisabet Melin and Annica Wallin, who tirelessly checked and proofread the English manuscript and made considerable improvements.
—and last but not least to Madelin Ahnlund for the amazing styling of the love food chapter!

Recipe Index